Golf My Way

by Jack Nicklaus

WITH KEN BOWDEN

Illustrations by Jim McQueen

SIMON AND SCHUSTER · NEW YORK

A Fireside Book
Published by Simon & Schuster, Inc.
A Division of Gulf & Western Corporation
Simon & Schuster Building
Rockefeller Center
1230 Avenue of the Americas
New York, New York 10020
FIRESIDE and colophon are registered trademarks
of Simon & Schuster, Inc.

ISBN 0-671-21702-X
ISBN 0-671-22278-3 Pbk.
Library of Congress Catalog Card Number 73-14090
Designed by Irving Perkins
Manufactured in the United States of America

35 34 33 32 31 30 29 28 27 26

Contents

PART TWO · DOWN THE FAIRWAY

PART THREE · AROUND AND ON THE GREEN

Foreword

by Jack Grout

Professional at La Gorce Country Club,
Miami Beach, Florida, and Jack Nicklaus'
one and only teacher

Strength, intelligence, an enormous capacity for hard work, and unswerving adherence to sound fundamentals are the factors behind Jack Nicklaus' fantastic successes as a golfer.

Strength may not be essential to play fine golf, but it is a priceless asset. The strong man can with comparative ease secure the height that is essential to carry the golf ball a long distance, and he also has the muscular capability to power the ball. These are critical factors at the highest reaches of the game, as is the stamina to practice and play day after day after day. It has been my privilege to observe or be associated with every great golfer of the twentieth century with the exception of Harry Vardon. Almost all of them were strong men. During my time in golf there have been some wonderful performances by men not gifted with great physical strength, but in the long haul they have run second to the powerful players. I believe that few men in the history of the game have possessed greater strength or more natural athletic ability than Jack Nicklaus.

Intelligence is necessary to a tournament golfer because the game is so difficult and inconstant that it can destroy anyone who lacks the capacity to control his emotions and to reason logically. Intelligence is necessary, too, in the acquisition of a profound knowledge of technique—profound enough to allow the player to be his own swing mechanic. The golfer who must fall back on a teacher every time any little thing sours in his game cannot but have

7

a limited future. Jack Nicklaus still likes to come to me every year for a checkup, but, beyond that, he has asked for my help only when he hasn't been able to solve a problem after weeks or months of intense personal study and work. Such occasions have been rare.

Today Jack plays such sensational golf with such apparent ease that many people who watch him probably gain the impression that his skills are heaven-sent rather than self-developed. That isn't true. No one ever worked harder at golf than Nicklaus during his teens and early twenties. At the age of ten, in his first year of golf, Jack must have averaged three hundred practice shots and at least eighteen holes of play daily. In later years, he would often hit double that number of practice shots and play thirty-six—even fifty-four— holes of golf a day during the summer. I have seen him practice for hours in rain, violent winds, snow, intense heat—nothing would keep him away from golf. Even a slight case of polio failed to prevent him from turning up at Scioto for a golf match. With this kind of dedication, and all his other assets, it would have been surprising if he had *not* become a great player.

However, I believe the most significant of all the factors that have contributed to Jack's success has been his unswerving adherence to sound swing fundamentals. It was my good fortune to be the professional at the Scioto Country Club in Columbus, Ohio, when this young man first became really keen on golf in 1950, and I take modest pride in having introduced him to many of the fundamentals that I consider to be the key to consistent play. But the credit for mastering those fundamentals, and for sticking to them through thick and thin, must go entirely to Jack. It is true that I have never had another pupil with so much natural talent for golf, or one so determined to excel at it. More significantly, I have never had another pupil who, once he was convinced about a fundamental, would so resolutely stick to it. The proof of that iron-willed commitment is to be seen in the fact that his basic swing is exactly the same today as it was fifteen years ago, when he won his first U. S. Amateur Championship at age nineteen. The benefits of it are evident in the present repetitiveness of his swing, and in the immense confidence he has in his technique today.

During forty years of teaching golf I have had a lot of naturally talented people pass through my hands. I feel I was able to help most of them, but none of the others progressed even halfway to what Nicklaus has achieved. I believe I can pinpoint a number of specific reasons why not.

First and probably foremost, the golf swing is, in my view, the most unnatural action in sport. It is extremely hard to teach, and even more difficult to learn. Consequently, unless a person has unusual amounts of ambition and dedication, the sheer difficulty of golf generally causes him to give it up long before he has attained his full potential at it.

Another reason there aren't too many budding Nicklauses to be found on the lesson tee is that most people take up golf too late in life. The ideal age for starting is in the early teens. And then, even when a really promising youngster comes along, you have to be realistic about the distractions he will face in relation to the amount of time and concentration golf demands. I have always insisted that youngsters should not take golf lessons until they are ready to concentrate—give the game their undivided attention and interest. I had no problem in this area with Jack. He was more single-minded about golf than any other youngster I've ever known has been about anything—even the opposite sex! For a very long period I don't think the young Nicklaus ever really thought about anything other than golf, and the better he became at it, the more he thought about it and the harder he was inspired to work at it.

However, I think the best clue to why Jack went on from where others with comparable natural talent have stopped lies in a brief sentence from his book *The Greatest Game of All*: "I was fortunate to learn the fundamentals at an early age." Jack and I both know countless promising golfers who have become hopelessly confused through failing to learn these fundamentals at the outset, usually with the result that they start confused and then compound the confusion by switching from method to method or from teacher to teacher, until eventually they end up trying to play a dozen different ways all at once. Jack never fell into that trap, and I believe that his evasion of it is one of the less-recognized factors behind his greatness.

It gives me much pleasure that Jack's fundamentalist approach to golf comes across so loud and clear in these pages, because my teaching has always been based on what I believe to be the time-proved fundamentals of the golf swing, even when such an approach has been unfashionable—as has been the case many times in my career. So far as I'm concerned, you can toss all the "tips" into the garbage can. The only way to play consistently good golf is through the mastery of a set of basics that the great players of the past have proved to be integral to the swing.

What are these basics? I don't want to steal the author's thunder by getting deeply involved in technique here. The basic points we worked on for so many long hours during those happy and productive years at Scioto will all be spread before you in these pages by the best pupil I ever had.

But there is another, nontechnical phase of the game that bears mention here, because I believe it had probably as great an effect on Jack's later career as did his efforts to develop sound technique.

Jack Nicklaus started to play competitive golf at a very early age, and it did wonders for him, as it has done for many other youngsters. Formal competition puts the game in clear perspective for a youngster, by giving meaning to what he is learning about technique. It causes him to become aware of the need for strategy, as well as fine shot-making; makes him realize that he will have to think well to win, not just swing well. It breeds maturity by thrusting him into pressurized situations and subjecting him to the emotions of success and failure. It builds self-confidence and self-reliance, and it helps a youngster to overcome nervousness. Most of all, in the majority of cases—certainly in Jack's—competition fires and sustains a youngster's enthusiasm for his sport, and breeds the development of goals and the dedication that leads to their attainment. I believe a lot of Jack's adult successes both on and off the golf course can be traced to the maturity and clear-headedness that grew out of his early competitive golfing experiences.

Finally, as a player and teacher of golf for forty years, I'd like to say a word to any readers of this fine book who have youngsters they'd like to think might follow in Jack Nicklaus' footsteps.

There have been thousands of boy and girl wonders in golf, but most of them have fallen apart before reaching adulthood. Why? I think the main reason is that they failed to learn sound basics during their early years, and thus held their games together to a certain point only through natural ability. As they grew older and the competition got tougher, this was not enough to carry them through.

I do not believe it is possible for any youngster, however naturally talented, to learn the fundamentals of golf in less than five years of dedicated effort, and even then I think that qualified personal guidance is essential if he is to reach his full potential. One of the great difficulties every golf professional encounters in teaching children to play the game is combating the misinformation given to them by their parents. By all means let a youngster read about golf, and encourage him especially to watch good players in the flesh and on television. But if you want him to play the game well, take him to a qualified teacher and resist the temptation to interfere with that teacher's program.

Jack Nicklaus was given that opportunity, and there was no doubt from the moment we began to work together that he would make the most of it. He was totally attentive, he asked intelligent questions, he had an infinite capacity for hard work, and his desire knew no bounds. He was certain to be a star. Even so, he never ceases to amaze me. I find his achievements astounding. There is no doubt that he is one of the greatest golfers of all time—possibly the greatest. It has been my privilege and joy to know him.

Introduction

I have written about golf before, but with the exception of my book *The Greatest Game of All,* written with the help of Herbert Warren Wind, which was largely autobiographical, I was offering tips on how to play. They derived from my own experiences that I felt at the time would be most likely to help others play better.

Why am I writing this book about golf? It's a fair question, and I'll give you an honest answer.

Thanks to a good helping of natural talent, a lot of assistance from a lot of people, much hard work, and a little luck, I've had a measure of success at golf. As a result, the game has been incredibly generous to me, in terms of both material possessions and personal happiness and fulfillment. Because of that, I have always had the urge to try to put something back into golf. For example, I hope that in building enjoyable golf courses I shall be able to make some small repayment of my great debt.

None of my previous books represents a really in-depth, A-to-Z description of how I play golf. Some people close to me have persuaded me that if I were to put this on record it would give pleasure, encouragement, and perhaps help to other lovers of the great game. This book is thus another small effort to repay my irredeemable debt to golf, and to the many people who have so wonderfully supported and encouraged me throughout my career.

My thanks are due to two people especially for their help with this book. Ken Bowden worked with me for many months on the research and writing. A low-handicap amateur as well as an internationally known golf writer, his knowledge of golf technique has been as valuable as his penmanship. Jim

McQueen, who has illustrated the book so beautifully, is also a fine player—in fact, away from the drawing board he's now head professional at one of my new golf courses. I am also most appreciative of the kind sentiments of my old friend and only tutor, Jack Grout, in his Foreword.

JACK NICKLAUS, 1973

PART ONE

Beliefs and Attitudes

CHAPTER 1

On Methods:
Mine and Others

I am not a believer in "methods." I'm a believer in fundamentals. Whatever any golfer does with a golf club should have only one purpose: to produce correct impact of club on ball. If he can achieve that consistently, the manner in which he does so doesn't really matter at all.

The more one studies or watches the good players of one's own day, the more apparent it becomes that the stars are basically alike in that their swings all possess certain fundamentals. For example, I cannot think of a great golfer who did not aim himself according to where he wanted the ball to go; or who did not turn his body on the backswing; or who did not swing, whether fast or slow, with a smooth tempo.

I know from my own experience how easy it is, in the search for self-improvement, to sacrifice fundamentals for gimmicks. When things are going badly at golf one suffers an almost irresistible urge to reach for a Band-Aid remedy. And, for a fellow who has limited time or opportunity to practice and play golf yet who is desperate for improvement, the promise offered by a "new" tip in a book or magazine, or the "new" method of a currently fashionable teaching pro, can be equally irresistible. I can understand that. Yet the hard facts are that any method, new or old, will fail if, first, it is not founded on sound fundamentals and, second, if the golfer trying to master it will not force or train or cajole himself into mastering those fundamentals before he attends to the frills.

I realize only too well how hard it is to resist gimmicks. Friends of mine who should know better will often remark to me at a tournament about the apparent variation in swing styles among tour players. Superficially it may seem to be the case. On the practice tee they'll watch Lee Trevino on one side of me and Doug Sanders on the other, and later will invite my comment on our "different" methods. Frequently their eye will have caught individual mannerisms or quirks rather than basics, such as a player's grip or setup to the ball.

Swing techniques of my fellow tour players really isn't a subject that turns me on; when I get away from the course I like to forget golf. Thus I've developed an answer for my friends that usually allows us to change the subject fairly quickly. "We may all get to impact a little differently," I'll say, "but *at* impact we're all the same—and impact is the bit that matters. If you'll watch a little more closely, I think you'll see this for yourself."

This is not really a conversational copout on my part. It is actually the crunch factor in any debate about method—I just bring it in a little early so that the talk may move to more interesting topics. The heart of the matter is that whatever style or shape or method of swinging a fellow adopts, if he can play golf at all, *during impact* he'll look pretty much like Lee Trevino, or Doug Sanders, or me, or any other good golfer you like to name. Whatever his legs, hips, hands, arms, shoulders, and head—and, above all, his club—may be doing at other points in the swing, they'll be much the same as ours just before, at, and just after impact.

It is this controlled, specific *impact* position that any method worth adopting *must* be designed to achieve. Keep that in mind as you read this or any other golf book, or listen to anyone talking golf technique. Good methods are not designed to produce precise angles of the wrists, or photogenic top-of-the-backswing postures, or perfect follow-throughs. These and other like factors may be important, but only as a route to a broader goal. That goal is a particular relationship of the golfer to his club, and through that of his club to the ball, at *impact*.

My own means of achieving this goal are, of course, distinctive. I have a very personal method of swinging the club. For example, although my method is designed to achieve exactly the same objective as Arnold Palmer's and Gary Player's and Lee Trevino's—to name three of my favorite adversaries—it is different from each of theirs both in over-all form and in particular components. It is very different, too, even from the methods of the two golfers

Always keep in mind that the ultimate objective of the golf swing is to produce square contact of club on ball. The overall swings of golfers like Ben Hogan, Bobby Jones and myself may appear different, but, because basically there is only one correct way to deliver the club to the ball, they look almost identical at impact.

who, as idols in different ways, most influenced my development as a player, Bob Jones and Ben Hogan.

How good is my method compared to theirs or to any other fine golfer's? Inevitably that question is asked in golf today, as is the question: "Who was the best-ever golfer?"

In all modesty, my answer is that I would not exchange my method of playing golf for any other golfer's, past or present, even if I could. I certainly don't claim perfection—I'm too frequently reminded of my imperfections on the course. Nor am I saying that there aren't facets of other players' games I envy: Sometimes I'd pay a king's ransom for Arnold's putting touch of ten years ago, or Gary's sand shots today, or that syrupy smooth Trevino body action through the ball when he's hot. But, all in all, I'm happy to stick with what I've got. I don't think I would have been a better player if I had learned to play another way. And I think I *will* be a better player yet if I can effect the improvements that I plan to make in my own method in the near future.

How does this preference for my own means of achieving the universal goal of correct impact relate to the average golfer? Am I inferring, by liking my own method best, that it would be best for him?

No, I am not. It would be presumptuous of me to suggest that my way is best for anyone else, for at least three reasons. First, Arnold, Gary, Lee, and a lot of other people frequently beat me. Second, there are some things about my game I wouldn't let my worst enemy steal, let alone hand to a struggling handicap player. Third, a golf swing isn't something that can be Xeroxed: Even if another golfer could pretty well reproduce my motions and tempo, it is far from certain he'd achieve the results I do.

What I will say, however, is this. There is a relatively easy and a relatively difficult way to achieve the common objective at golf—which, let me remind you yet again, is not a particular pattern of swing but proper impact of club on ball. I believe that my style is closer to the relatively easy way than it is to the relatively difficult way. I think that my style is easier to learn initially and to play with fruitfully as the years advance. In that sense I'd certainly be happy for my game to serve as a model—but only as a rough model, mind you, not as a working blueprint.

To me, the relatively easy way to play golf is with a swing in which the clubface starts square to the ball, gradually opens (turns clockwise) as it goes back, and gradually closes (turns counterclockwise) as it returns, until, at impact, it is again square to the ball. This opening and closing is neither excessive nor contrived, but simply the natural response to a one-piece takeaway, a generous turn of the body, a free swing of the arms and a reflexive hinging or cocking of the wrists on the backswing, and a reciprocal set of

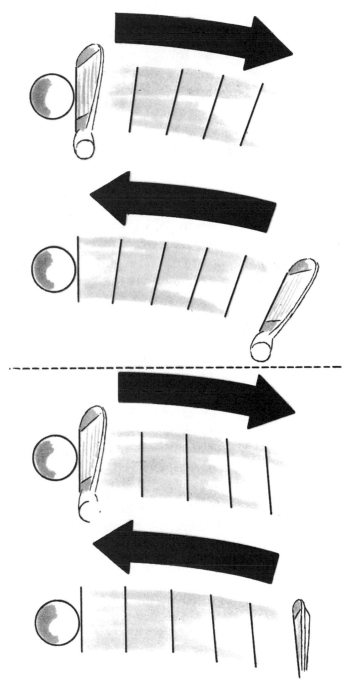

The thin vertical lines in these drawings represent clubface alignment during the takeaway and the approach to impact. History would seem to favor the open-to-closed pattern of clubface movement (top illustration) over the closed-to-open pattern (lower illustration). Harry Vardon, Walter Hagen, Bobby Jones, Gene Sarazen, Sam Snead, and, at his peak, Ben Hogan were open-to-closed players. Arnold Palmer and Lee Trevino are the only two superstars who have played primarily with a closed-to-open action.

actions on the forward swing. It is my impression that the golfer who plays this way usually has a fairly upright plane, a wide arc, and a high backswing and follow-through. His tempo more often than not is smooth, and his actions seem to flow nicely into one graceful whole. If he is a good player, his swing is obviously finely controlled. Yet there is often about it an element of abandon, or freedom, in the way the club releases through the ball: almost as though it were whistling along of its own volition. Over-all, to me, this open-to-closed type of golfer makes the game look graceful, physically "easy"—sometimes, you might say, almost symphonic. There rarely appears to be much stress or strain about his manner of striking the ball.

The relatively difficult way to play golf, as I see it, is with a swing in which the clubface habitually closes (turns counterclockwise) as it goes back and opens (turns clockwise) on its return to find squareness at the ball. Again, these movements may not be excessive, but to me the resulting complete swing often looks more contrived, forced, less natural. I associate this kind of swing with a flattish plane, a restricted arc and either a blocked or chopped-off finish. The tempo sometimes seems to be wooden, staccato. There is often an air of intense, even strained, physical control about the whole pattern of movement. I sense that the club is being maneuvered rather than flung or whipped or whistled through the ball; that the golfer is pulling back rather than releasing the clubhead. Over-all, the shut-to-open type of golfer makes the game, to me, look more difficult than it actually is. His swing seems to punish him physically more than necessary.

Great golf has been played with both of these methods, and will be in the future. But there can be no doubt as to which method history favors. Harry Vardon was an open-to-closed player. So were Walter Hagen and Bob Jones. So are Gene Sarazen and Sam Snead: the one, now in his seventies, playing three or four times a week and regularly shooting par at his home course; the other, in his sixties, finishing high in the money on tour just about every time he tees it up. Ben Hogan's midcareer swing change made him a more open-to-closed golfer, and he won his greatest victories in his forties. Arnold Palmer was predominantly a shut-faced golfer in his early days, but as he's aged and lost a little of his immense strength, Arnold has moved toward a more open-faced action and struck the ball, by his own admission, better for it.

Although I deliberately play some shots with a shut-faced swing, I am basically an open-to-square-to-closed golfer. The reason is that I believe this type of swing is the simplest in concept, is the easiest to control, is the most natural to perform anatomically, requires the least strength, needs the least practice, and will best stand the test of time.

(Why not, you may well ask, play with a square-faced action. Well, I haven't read anything about the so-called "square methods"—I've never read a golf instruction book or article in my life. But as I interpret what I've heard about these theories, they mean that the clubface remains square to the target line and the ball throughout the swing. Maybe if someone could show me how it's possible to do that in an action involving a large arc and a tilted plane, and still swing the clubhead through the ball at 120 mph, I'd try it. Until then, I simply don't believe it's possible.)

Of the outstanding golfers on tour today, Lee Trevino is the most pronouncedly shut-faced player. I have great admiration for his game, particularly his gracefulness through the ball. But it is my guess that in seven or eight years Lee will either have changed his style or won't be winning like he is today. Trevino's method demands great strength and bodily agility, not to mention very precise timing and superb coordination. All these attributes must decline a little with age. Lee, in fact, exemplifies the major difficulty of the shut-faced player when he admits, very freely, that he can play only when his legs are feeling good and working perfectly. The reason is technically very simple: The more closed the clubface coming into the ball, the more the legs must work to keep the body ahead of it, to prevent either a pull or pull-hook.

I believe that Trevino's present method derives from his long battle with a bad hook (the main reason that he was so long getting out onto the tour). Lee simply had to discover a way to keep the clubface open at impact or give up golf. My guess is that eventually he found it easier to do this by working from a closed clubface coming from the top than by setting and holding a slightly open clubface position from the top, as I do when playing my bread-and-butter fade. But his type of action is rarely to be seen on tour, despite what the technical analysts among our writing friends sometimes believe they observe. I said in a newspaper column recently that 90 percent of the current tour golfers play open-to-closed to a greater or lesser degree, and I'll stick to that assertion.

So much for comparison of methods. The basic point I want to make is that there are certain fundamentals common to *all* successful methods of swinging a golf club, and it is with these that the ambitious golfer should concern himself, not with the mannerisms of any one player no matter how successful that player may be. Even when you have more or less mastered these fundamentals, I can assure you that you'll still have plenty on your hands keeping them in good working order without complicating the issue by copying other people's idiosyncrasies.

If there is one thing I have learned during my years as a professional, it is that the only constant thing about golf is its inconstancy. As an amateur there were times when I believed that if only I didn't have to clean up my room, or get an education, or earn a living, I would be able to hone my game to a point of absolute perfection and then hold it there permanently. I grew up in the era of Hogan. Everything I saw of him and read of him and heard of him indicated that he had achieved utter mechanical perfection in the striking of a golf ball. Perfect repetition. Flawless automation. This was my dream. All I needed to achieve it was sufficient time to work at my game.

I was kidding myself. When I turned professional, suddenly I had all the time and opportunity I needed. And I discovered, fast, that my dream was just that: a dream. No matter how much work I did, one week I would have it and the next I couldn't hit my hat.

This is still true today. I am a far better golfer than when I started out on the tour twelve years ago, and I feel that I have improved to some degree each year. But that is more the result of maturity and competitive experience than of improvement in the mechanics of my game. All I can claim in terms of "perfecting" my method is that I now hit a higher percentage of shots the way I plan them than I did twelve years ago, or even two years ago. Yet I still rarely get through one tournament using the same swing thoughts, or "feels," that got me through the last one. The basics of my swing don't change, but the mental pictures I need to keep it oiled and running smoothly certainly do. For example, I played the 1972 U. S. and British Opens, three weeks apart, with totally different mental swing pictures, or "pegs." Sometimes my key thoughts will change from round to round, or even in midround if something about my game dissatisfies me. And on the putting greens I can become a real chameleon, making small adjustments to some part of my set-up or stroke from hole to hole.

The point I want to make as emphatically as possible right at the start of this book is that you cannot automate the golf swing. No "method" of swinging the club has ever been invented that will enable a golfer to achieve machine-like shot-making perfection over an extended period, and in my opinion none ever will be—certainly not by Jack Nicklaus.

I believe the best a fellow can do to forge himself a good golf game is to select those fundamentals that have been common to the greatest number of good players down the years, then apply them as assiduously as his talent, opportunity, and desire allow. Of course, if he happened to end up swinging like Jack Nicklaus I'd be delighted.

Not very consoling words, I'll agree. But honest ones. And if there's one thing golf demands above all else, it's honesty.

CHAPTER 2

It Helps to Know Where—
and How—You Want to Go

You will very rarely see a professional hit a long shot straight—absolutely dead straight, I mean. The ball may seem to fly relatively straight a lot of times, but if you watch carefully, from behind the player, you'll see that it generally turns either left or right toward the end of its flight. The bend may be fractional—often no more than a *suggestion* of draw or fade. But it's there on 99 percent of even the best players' longer shots.

Anytime any golfer hits a ball perfectly straight with a big club it is, in my view, a fluke, an accident. Maybe "miracle" would be a better word. How so? Well, let's have a look at what actually happens at impact on those rare occasions when I hit a solid drive dead straight:

1. The clubhead is traveling at about 120 mph.
2. The clubhead is moving directly along my target line—and I mean *exactly,* not even a fraction of an inch across the line.
3. The clubface is perfectly square to the target—not turned even a shade left or right.
4. The ball is hit on the center of the clubface—not a hair toward the heel or toe.

Those are the mechanical requirements for an absolutely straight golf shot. And even if you meet them, you've generally still got a wind factor to beat. Makes golf sound impossible, doesn't it!

I think golf would be impossible for me if I tried to achieve what I've just described on every full shot I play. The reason, obviously, is that I'd never know where the ball was going on the ninety-nine out of a hundred occasions when it didn't fly dead straight. One time it would go to the right, the next to the left. And I could never be sure how *much* to the left or the right. I'd be playing a guessing game with myself on every hole. I'd be a straitjacket case in no time flat.

Good golf demands the ability to play percentage shots, by which I mean consistently bringing the ball to the target either from left to right or from right to left. To fly the ball thus one must know exactly what will make it curve as planned. This demands knowledge of spin. Attempting to build a golf game without a thorough understanding of spin is like trying to fly without having learned about the plane's controls. Even if you get off the ground, you're going to have a sticky ride and a bumpy landing.

I don't suppose I have thought consciously about golf's fundamental cause-and-effect factors—the spin factors—since I was a kid. In fact, I can't remember ever learning them in a formal sort of way; they must have just seeped into my consciousness through experience during my early teens. They are certainly so obvious to me, and I apply them so automatically in my own game today, that I wasn't even going to write about them in this book. Then, in thinking more deeply about the matter, it occurred to me how many mature golfers—mature in years, I mean—probably do not fully understand cause and effect. For instance, only a few weeks ago I got into a discussion with a pro-am partner about his slice, a really wicked monster that was obviously ruining his golfing life. He'd tried just about every method and gimmick ever invented. But what he'd obviously failed to comprehend were the simple, basic mechanics of impact—what causes a ball to fly a certain way. He was forever changing his swing without really considering what he wanted it to achieve for him at impact. Thus I now feel it's worth taking a moment to look at the possibly elementary, but apparently often overlooked, spin factors in golf.

Assuming there is no wind, the superdrive I've just described will fly straight because the ball starts along the target line and carries only pure backspin. To picture this type of spin, think of the ball as having a stripe around its equator, which is set vertical to the target line at address. As this ball spins in flight during the supershot, that stripe will remain absolutely vertical.

Should I apply sidespin (as well as backspin) to the ball, however, the stripe will deviate from the vertical and the flight path of the ball will curve. If I hit the ball so that the top of the stripe is inclined left of the target, the ball will curve left in the air. If I hit the ball so that the top of the stripe is inclined right

TOPSPIN PRODUCES GROUND BALL

A word here on backspin. It is essential to raise and hold the ball in the air. It's a fallacy that a good golf shot is ever hit with topspin or overspin. A ball so hit always dives quickly to earth—if it ever gets off the ground in the first place.

of the target, the ball will curve right in the air. The more sidespin I apply—the more the stripe deviates from vertical—the more the ball will curve one way or the other during its flight. In all instances the curve will be most noticeable near the end of the ball's flight, as the decrease in backspin allows the sidespin to take greater effect.

What causes this sidespin? The simple answer is *any kind of glancing or crosscutting blow*. And what causes a glancing or crosscutting blow? No, it isn't the fact that you didn't turn enough going back or failed to start the downswing with your legs. What's more, it isn't necessarily what you've come to believe from reading other golf books: that an inside-out swing *always* causes a hook, or that an outside-in swing *always* produces a slice. *At root,* it's the fact that, at impact, *your clubface was not looking in the same direction as your clubhead was traveling*.

To make this clearer yet, let's specifically relate the interaction of clubface alignment and swing path to the curve balls and foul balls you actually hit on the course:

WHEN YOU SLICE. Your clubface is looking *right* of the direction in which your clubhead is moving. Thus you cut across the ball from out to in, imparting left-to-right sidespin to the ball.

WHEN YOU FADE. The same crosscutting action as above, only the angle between your clubface and swing path is smaller.

WHEN YOU HOOK. Your clubface is looking *left* of the direction in which your clubhead is moving. Thus you cut across the ball from in to out, imparting right-to-left sidespin to the ball.

WHEN YOU DRAW. Same crosscutting action as when you hook, only the angle between your clubface and swing path is smaller.

WHEN YOU PULL STRAIGHT LEFT. Your clubface is looking in the same direction as the clubhead is traveling. The trouble is that you're swinging from

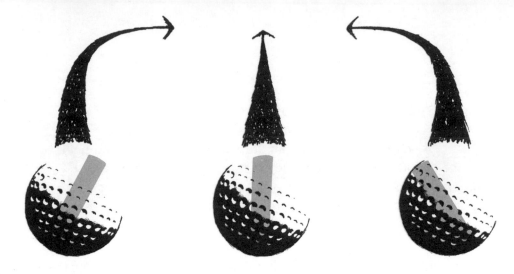

Failure to clearly comprehend the cause and effect of sidespin limits many a golfer's progress. When at impact the club's face looks in the same direction the head of the club is traveling, the ball spins on a vertical equator and thus flies straight (center illustration). When the club's face looks to the right of the direction in which the head is traveling, the ball spins around an equator tilted from left to right and thus curves to the right during flight (left illustration). When the club's face looks to the left of the direction in which the head is traveling, the ball spins around an equator tilted from right to left and thus curves to the left during flight (right illustration). Understanding how most foul balls result from a mismatching of clubface alignment and clubhead path at impact is basic to building a strong golf game.

out to in, across your target line. (Consequently, a golfer who hits *straight* left should not think of himself as a hooker, but recognize that he actually has a slicer's fault—an out-to-in swing path.)

WHEN YOU PUSH STRAIGHT RIGHT.   Your clubface is looking in the same direction as the clubhead is traveling. The problem is that you are swinging from in to out across your target line. (Thus, although the ball ends up to the right, like a slicer's, you are actually swinging on a hooker's path.)

WHEN YOU PULL-HOOK (the ball starts left and curves more left).   Your clubhead is traveling from out to in, across the target line, with the clubface looking *left* of the swing path.

WHEN YOU PUSH-SLICE (the ball starts right and curves more right).   Your clubhead is traveling from in to out, across the target line, with the clubface looking *right* of the swing path.

Elementary? To a good player, probably. To a high handicapper, I'm not so sure. Either way, the basic point may be worth restating: It helps to know where—and how—you want to go before you start going there.

CHAPTER 3

Why I Always Played the Fade— and Now Sometimes Play the Draw

There is a tactical as well as a technical reason why the intelligent golfer rarely, if ever, tries to hit the ball dead straight. Suppose a pin were sitting in the center of a green, leaving you with 30 feet of putting surface on either side. If you tried to hit the ball straight to the pin but sliced it 20 feet off line, you'd leave yourself a 20-foot putt. But your tendency—or, in my case, usually my preference—is to fade the ball. Thus you aim 10 feet left of the hole. If you now hit the ball straight you will have a 10-foot putt. If you slice the ball 20 feet you'll still only have a 10-foot putt.

This is percentage golf, a part of golf in which the mind must rule the muscles. The example I give applies on any golf shot you hit through the air, and it applies whether you choose, or are naturally inclined, to fade or draw the ball. It is as important a factor in compiling consistently good scores as any element of your equipment, your setup, or your swing.

As I said in the previous chapter, to play percentage golf you must be able to determine how you want to spin the ball, and to what degree, and then do what you've planned on a high proportion of shots. But that is stage 3 in effectively flighting the ball. Stage 1 is making a basic policy decision about which way you should, or can, basically play the game—your options, of course, are to play either from left to right or from right to left. Stage 2 is developing and habitualizing a pattern of swing based on that decision.

I have preferred to flight the ball left to right virtually since I started golf. Looking back, there are some good reasons for this. First, I think, was the influence of Ben Hogan on my golf thinking as a youngster. Bob Jones—predominantly a right-to-left player—was always the golfer whose record I most wanted to emulate, but as I grew up I wanted more and more to do it Hogan's way. I grew up at a time when Ben preferred to fade the ball, and I was awed by the authority and consistency of his shot-making. In terms of technique, he stood high on a pinnacle in my adolescent mind. Another factor that shaped my game must have been the conditions under which I learned to play golf. We had little wind and a lot of well-watered turf at Scioto, two conditions encouraging those high-flying, quick-stopping shots that the left-to-right pattern produces. Yet another factor was that the considerable time I spent getting out of Scioto's lush rough encouraged an upright, open-bladed attack on the ball. Then there was the fact that all the out-of-bounds areas at Scioto are on the left, making a fade a safer shot than a draw. Certainly Jack Grout's insistence that I hit the ball high had a strong influence on my game. He believed that to win tournaments a golfer had to be able to consistently carry the ball high through the air even with the longer, less-lofted clubs. To him, a high-flying, soft-landing shot was also a yardstick of powerful and accurate striking. As a kid who loved to see a well-hit drive or long-iron hang in the air and then fall dead and stop smack on target, I readily agreed.

Yet another factor encouraging my making left-to-right shots was the type of trajectory I came to favor as my game developed. There are differences —in distance and stopping power—between a shot that starts out high and curves back to earth on much the same trajectory, and a shot hit hard enough to start low, then soar to a peak and drop back to earth almost vertically. As time went on I was able to hit the ball hard enough to achieve this soaring kind of trajectory with the longer clubs. It helped me to achieve distance; but most of all, I loved the way the ball fell "dead" to the ground, and the finer control over shot placement that this trajectory allowed.

I suppose my distance capability was the biggest single factor in shaping my left-to-right flight preference. Because from the outset I had little difficulty in achieving good distance, it rarely was necessary for me to hook the ball to reach the long par 4s or even the par 5s. This is not to say that I always reached them—I often missed by miles. But the *capability* was there, even when fading the ball.

The result of all these factors was that by the time I was age thirteen or fourteen, I hated to hook—or even draw—the ball. Increasingly I came to see it as the wilder way to play golf. I'd get so mad if I moved the ball 5 feet right to left in the air with a driver, I'd slam the club to the ground. After all, Hogan didn't hit shots like that!

I think I can honestly say that I did not once depart from my basic policy of fading the ball in tournament play from the time I won my first away-from-home tournament at thirteen in 1953 (the Ohio State Junior, thirteen-to-fifteen-

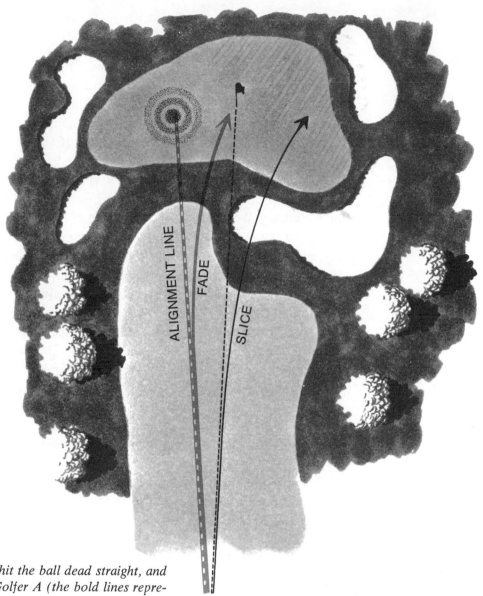

Good golfers rarely try to hit the ball dead straight, and this drawing shows why. Golfer A (the bold lines represent his strategy) prefers to fade the ball. Here he aims 10 feet left of the pin. If he executes perfectly the fade he has planned (and his distance is spot on), the ball will finish in the hole. If he hits the ball dead straight, he has a 10-foot putt. If he inadvertently doubles the amount of fade he has planned, he still has only a 10-foot putt. On the other hand, Golfer B (lines not shown) attempts to hit the ball dead straight on all his shots. Here he goes for the pin. If he succeeds, well and good. But if he slices the ball that same double degree as Golfer A, he faces a 20-foot putt. Thus, assuming equal imperfection in stroke execution through eighteen holes, Golfer B will be putting from twice Golfer A's distance on every green.

year-old division, with 161 for 36 holes), until I shot 79-73 in the opening rounds of the Lucky International in San Francisco early in 1963, missing the cut and the prize money for the first time in my professional career. Through that ten-year period, while playing predominantly left to right, I had won two U. S. Amateur Championships (1959 and 1961), the U. S. Open (1962), and had finished third in the money list in my first year on tour (1962) with over $60,000. There had been little reason to change the pattern.

However, on the eve of the Lucky International I got an attack of bursitis in my left hip. We can pass over the details of the ailment and its eventual relief, except to say that it forced me to change my game. Simply to prevent hurting myself too badly, I had to slow down my hip action through the ball. Any time you do that your hands and arms are going to close the clubface sooner, making it very difficult to fade the ball. I absolutely couldn't—at least not consistently. For the first time in my life I was obliged to play with a right-to-left draw.

As the Masters drew near that year, I was able to convince myself that this was not all bad. I had by then won the Desert Classic in Palm Springs basically hitting my shots right to left, and I had often thought that of all the major championship courses we play in America, Augusta National most favored a right-to-left game. Now was the time to find out if I was right. And apparently I was, because, despite some pain from the hip, I won the Masters that year—its youngest winner ever—with a score of 286, beating Tony Lema by one shot.

The hip problem—which hasn't recurred, thank goodness—lasted about three months, and, combined with the Masters win, it gave me a new dimension on myself. I learned that I could do something that I had never tried to do before: play successful golf from right to left.

Looking back now, I'm almost grateful for that bursitis flare-up. If it had never happened I doubt that I would ever have changed my method. And if I hadn't I wouldn't be as good a player as I am today.

What the experience gave me was enough confidence to try to adapt my basic shot-making pattern to each particular course or set of conditions. At first this required fairly extensive periods of turn-around work on my game each time I changed "shapes." I would, for example, have to spend two or three weeks before each Masters working on the setup and swing changes required to switch from a fade to draw. It was also necessary to go through a "debriefing" phase after such a change to retrieve my left-to-right pattern. And it didn't always work, as my Masters record and other periods of my career prove. Sometimes I'd think I had the new shape down pat, only to find in the tournament that it needed more work. I'd then find myself in an irritatingly indecisive frame of mind, which would usually force me to play defensively and thus poorly.

There was another period, 1968–70, when, through a combination setup and takeaway fault, I was again in a position where to hit the ball halfway decently I virtually *had* to draw it. I did win the U. S. Open at Baltusrol in 1967 (after failing to make the cut in my defense of the Masters title), but I was an inconsistent golfer if you look at my record for the next three years. I didn't win another "major" until the 1970 British Open. In fact, the "forced draw" problem continued on and off right through until late in 1970, when I finally diagnosed—and hopefully permanently cured—the technical faults that were causing it.

KNOW HOW FAR YOU HIT EACH CLUB

Throughout this chapter I have basically been discussing trajectory in a lateral sense. Equally important in tournament golf is control of trajectory longitudinally—distance and height. I am probably laboring a point if I say that you will never even begin to score consistently well until you know exactly how far you can hit the ball with each club under varying conditions, but it is surprising how many golfers don't. Even if you already strike the ball reasonably well, just a little more care in this area might further improve your scores.

Here, for example, are my distances with each club under normal conditions:

Driver:	250 yards and up
3-wood:	235 yards and up
1-iron:	215–235 yards
2-iron:	205–220 yards
3-iron:	195–210 yards
4-iron:	185–200 yards
5-iron:	170–185 yards
6-iron:	155–170 yards
7-iron:	140–155 yards
8-iron:	130–145 yards
9-iron:	105–135 yards
Pitching wedge:	80–130 yards
Sand wedge:	Up to 100 yards

Why not chart your game similarly?

Playing percentage golf demands the ability to consistently fade or draw the ball. Which "shape" a golfer chooses must depend on his strength and his natural swing tendencies. Shots drawn right to left fly lower and run farther than shots faded from left to right, and thus offer distance advantages to weaker players. Because they fly higher and come to rest faster than drawn shots, faded shots generally offer powerful players greater ball control. The ideal, of course, is to be able to move the ball either way at will to meet each specific shot-making challenge.

Moving my home from Columbus, Ohio, to North Palm Beach in Florida also helped to round out my shot-shaping education. It is a rare day on the east coast of Florida when the wind doesn't blow some. When it becomes more than a breeze on as big a course, say, as the East at the old PGA National, a draw—flying under the wind and fighting it—is a mighty useful shot.

Playing and practicing in Florida wind these past four years has enabled me to finish off what the hip problem started; that plus, of course, the all-

AN IMPORTANT HEIGHT FACTOR

Another factor you must consider in developing an effective game is height. I believe that the climatic and golf course conditions we experience most of the year on the majority of American courses encourage high-flying, quick-stopping shots. Height results from a square-faced or even slightly open-faced impact, which is best achieved with a relatively upright swing plane. I hope I'm not overselling my own style of play, but I do feel that this is an important point to consider in molding a golf game.

around improvement in my game that naturally resulted from greater maturity and experience. Today I can fade or draw at will, as the weather or the topography of a hole dictates. The shots don't always come off, of course, but then neither did my fade when it was my whole armory. That's golf. At least I now have the knowledge and confidence to try to play from "both sides of the course" that I certainly lacked during my first fifteen years at the game.

Probably better than anything, the first three major championships of 1972 indicated how far I'd come. Although in the Masters, because the fairways were unusually hard and fast, I played a greater number of faded shots in 1972 than in some other years, I basically drew the ball, as I have at Augusta since 1963. In the U. S. Open at Pebble Beach I basically faded the ball, having felt from the first time I played this magnificent course as an amateur that it is most susceptible to that shape of shot, even in as strong a wind as we had on the last round in 1972. In the first three rounds of the 1972 British Open I tried to "caress" my scores from the course with a fade, because Muirfield poses for me much more of an accuracy than a distance problem. This policy had worked when I won there in 1966. But I was not playing well in the 1972 British Open, and in the final round, with much more to gain than I could lose, I decided to make a setup change that I felt was necessary to allow me to hit the ball more solidly. It produced, as I knew it would, a draw; and it very nearly saved the day for me. With the exception of two shots—the tee shots at the par-3 sixteenth and par-5 seventeenth holes—I played, tee to green, my best golf ever in the final round of a major championship. Despite the final result (second), I was very satisfied with what that round signaled in terms of the evolution of the Nicklaus golf game.

CHAPTER 4

Some Plane Truth

The ideal way to play golf would be to swing the club in a vertical plane—like a pendulum. That way your club would never deviate from your target line, and, assuming you could also devise a way to keep the clubface square to the target, you'd be bound to hit every shot straight.

If this is true, then the *least* ideal way to play golf would be with a horizontal swing—the baseball-type action. That way the club would be moving in the direction you wanted to hit the ball only at the split second when the circle the club describes meets your target line.

Obviously both these extremes are physical impossibilities, but I mention them to illustrate, in a nutshell, why I prefer an upright swing plane. It seems to me that the less I move the club off the target line—or the longer I keep it *near* to the target line—the better my chance of swinging the clubhead along the target line at impact. The closer to vertical my swing plane, the longer the club will be near the target line.

My swing plane is nowhere near vertical, of course, but it is definitely and purposely upright. I make a deliberate effort to both turn my shoulders and swing my arms on an upright path in the backswing.

A few months ago I had an interesting discussion with John Jacobs, the distinguished British teaching professional, on the question of an upright versus a flat swing plane. John seems to believe that American golfers on the whole, and certainly our Walker Cup amateurs of 1971 and some of our younger professionals, are tending toward too upright a swing plane. He calls the tendency,

SAME SWING WITH EVERY CLUB

While I'm on this subject, let me make another point about swing "geometry" (to borrow a word as well as a thought from John Jacobs).

Get it out of your head—if it was ever in there—that you deliberately have to make a different kind of swing with each club. Certainly in terms of plane, you should feel like you are making the same basic swing with every club in the bag (except, of course, your putter). Whatever differences do in fact occur will do so automatically as a result of shaft length. Your arc decreases with the shorter clubs, and your plane becomes more upright as, of necessity, you move closer to the ball.

with his tongue in his cheek, "The American Disease." And he's inclined to blame me for it, in the sense that whatever successes I've had have established me as a model for the whole nation!

Jacobs argues that, although an upright swing plane may well improve a golfer's accuracy by allowing him to keep the club nearer the target line through the ball, it can often rob him of distance by (1) restricting his body turn or pivot and (2) making it difficult for him to sweep solidly into the back of the ball rather than chop down on it (obviously the flatter the swing plane, the longer the club is at ball level).

John's point may be valid for some golfers, but I'm going to have to say that it isn't in my case. The reason the argument doesn't hold water for me is that my upright plane is combined with a very full, very wide swing arc. I'm told by the technical analysts at *Golf Digest* magazine that relative to my height (5 feet 11½ inches) I have the longest clubhead arc of any successful golfer on tour. I can well believe it, because achieving the widest possible arc has been a fundamental of my game since Jack Grout drummed its importance deep into my soul more than twenty years ago at Scioto. And the critical point is that it would be impossible for me to achieve this big arc without a very full body turn in the backswing.

I think this is a factor that anyone who feels inclined to copy my style of swing should understand very clearly. You must make a wide arc if you hope to capitalize from an upright plane. A golfer who swings the club on an up-

An upright plane gives the golfer his best chance of swinging the club along the target line at impact. However, uprightness of plane must be accompanied by width of arc if the swing is to pack power, and if this power is to be transformed into yardage through solid delivery of the clubhead into the back of the ball. In attempting to swing upright for good direction, many golfers lose distance by merely lifting the club with the hands and arms, instead of making the backswing a fully extended coiling and stretching of the body. Loss of leverage and a weak, sharply downward, chopping clubhead delivery usually result.

MY NONFLYING RIGHT ELBOW

I'm often accused of having a "flying" right elbow. It's a false assertion. To achieve the degree of uprightness I want, and also the width of arc I seek, my right elbow has to come well away from my side on the backswing. But the elbow is not "flying." To do so it would have to be pointed outward—behind me. If it did that, my club would point across the target line at the top of the backswing and I could never swing back into the ball correctly. My right elbow may be high, but it is actually pointed downward toward the ground at the top of the swing, from where it correctly brushes close to my right side on the forward swing.

right plane but with a narrow arc is obviously going to lack power, because his action will be a lifting up of the club with his hands and arms rather than a full coiling of his body. That sort of movement certainly isn't going to move the ball far out of your shadow. It is a lazy way to play golf, and one that virtually eliminates the forward swing leverage from which real clubhead speed derives.

Possibly Jacobs has observed this kind of action in many of his apparently too-upright pupils, and has found an effective cure to be a flatter plane, which I agree can help many a golfer to make a fuller body turn, and may also help him to return the club at ball level through impact. But frankly, although I'm

FOLLOW-THROUGH PLANE SHOULD MATCH
BACKSWING PLANE

If you have an upright backswing, you should have an upright follow-through. If you have a flat backswing, you should have a flat follow-through. If you don't, you are changing planes in midstream, which is bound to breed inconsistency.

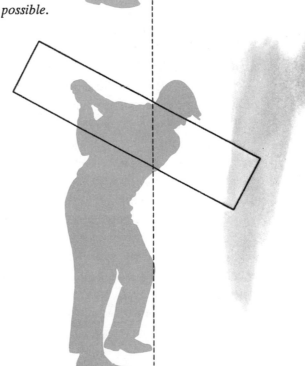

These silhouettes drawn from photographs of Ben Hogan and myself probably represent the practical limits of "flat" and "upright" golf swings. Most top golfers swing on a plane somewhere between these two extremes, but if there is a trend among modern tournament players it is toward swinging on an upright plane to keep the club as close to the target line as possible for as long as possible.

FORWARD SWING ARC STEEPER THAN BACKSWING ARC

Don't make the common mistake of believing that the club's arc on the forward swing should reproduce exactly its backswing arc. Correct lower-body movement (toward the target) on the forward swing, combined with delayed uncocking of the wrists, causes the clubhead to descend to the ball on a *steeper* arc than that on which it went back.

Among some good golfers—Gary Player is a fine example —these forward swing actions also tend to make the plane of the forward swing a little flatter than the backswing plane. If that happens in your swing, be glad. It is fine insurance against swinging the clubhead out beyond the target line before impact.

not a teacher, I'd only go along with making a golfer swing flatter if he or she was really poorly equipped in a muscular or coordinative sense (and then big distance with *any* kind of swing plane is unlikely). To me, the accuracy factor of the upright plane is too valuable to be easily discarded. Before I did flatten anyone's plane, I'd want to see if he couldn't first increase his power by extending and widening his backswing arc while retaining an upright plane.

It's difficult for me to comment on the effectiveness of the flat-plane type of swing because, except when I've been under a tree or otherwise restricted, I've never used one. I have no real idea what such an action feels like, although I've seen plenty of them work pretty well: Hogan, Palmer, Player, and Trevino are all relatively flat swingers.

However, one factor that any golfer must certainly take into account in determining his swing plane is his physique. If you're built like a Harlem Globetrotter, you're going to have to stand relatively close to the ball, which will naturally cause your swing plane to be on the upright side. By flattening it you simply add an *unnatural* complication to an already complex game. The reverse applies if you're built like a jockey; your physical necessity to stand taller and farther away from the ball will naturally flatten your swing plane. Either way, you must find a way to live with what's natural to you.

CHAPTER 5

The Motive Force: Leverage=Centrifugal Force= Clubhead Speed=Distance

I am known as a fairly long hitter. How do I do it?

Well, let me say first off that the most important word is "hit." Sure, I swing the club to achieve the hit, but I do *hit* through the ball—and think of hitting through the ball—very hard; often, on a drive, with just about everything I can muster. I've never believed all that stuff about "let the clubhead do the work." If you want the ball to go a long way, you've got to hit it hard. You've got to *make,* not let, the clubhead work.

Like Arnold Palmer—who's still no patsy off the tee, despite those glasses and gray hairs—I was taught to hit the ball hard from the day I first picked up a golf club. Jack Grout encouraged me to spend a lot of my practice time swinging all-out with scant regard to where the ball went. In common with Arnold's teacher, his father Deacon, Grout believed that a golfer who learns to swing hard initially can usually acquire accuracy later, whereas a golfer who gets too accuracy-conscious at the outset will rarely be able to make himself hit the ball hard later on. It's a philosophy that I think Arnie would agree has contributed to both our successes. Because, believe me, whatever arguments those short knockers may throw at you, distance is a huge

CENTRIFUGAL FORCE AND HAND ACTION

Centrifugal force is an interesting factor In golf. I was told just after the 1972 World Series at Firestone Country Club, by someone who should know, that in a powerful swing the club-head speed deriving from centrifugal force becomes so great by the time the club is about hip high on the forward swing that the golfer's problem is not really to accelerate the club further, but simply to go along with it in such a way that he doesn't check its velocity. I told my scientific informant that even if this is true I distinctly have the feeling that I do accelerate the club right through the ball on full shots. He felt this was correct, in that if you don't at least *feel* you're accelerating throughout the forward swing there's a possibility you're actually holding something back.

But his theory seems to explain a shot I hit at the par-3 fifteenth in the second round at Firestone. The choice of club lay between a two-iron and three-iron, and I decided to go with an easy two-iron. Coming into the ball I was deliberately "soft" with my hands. I've never hit a better two-iron in my life! The ball finished *over* the green.

Maybe this explains what happens on those good drives where I often have a "soft" feeling in my hands through the ball. You could say that my hand action on such shots was merely a *reaction* to the earlier accelerative effects of centrifugal force on the clubhead generated by proper leverage. My hands merely went along for the ride. It's an interesting possibility. All I know is I wish it happened more often.

asset in golf. I certainly encourage my own boys to swing hard *through* the ball and, thankfully, they seem to have my kind of appetite for it.

With that over-all philosophy in mind, I'd like to discuss the factors that I believe create the very high clubhead speed required to hit the ball a long way.

I'm fully aware of the specific actions I perform physically during the swing, and I will tell you about them in detail in later chapters. But I'm not

THE TRUTH ABOUT MY HANDS

I am asked questions about my hands almost as often as I'm asked to sign autographs. I have stubby hands with short fingers. I wear a men's small golf glove. Actually my wife, Barbara, has stronger hands than mine from doing the dishes. That's why I always have to pass a tight jar lid over to her. Knowing that, you won't be surprised to learn that I regard as bunk that hoary old maxim about big, strong hands being essential for good golf.

too hot on the terms that scientists or engineers might use in analyzing the golf swing. In fact, I shall never forget, when writing a previous book, spending the better part of three days fumbling for some sort of definition of the golf swing within a mechanical framework. I never achieved one that really satisfied me, and I certainly haven't played the worse for my inability to do so. But I make this point because I shall have to use a couple of words in this chapter that have specific technical meanings, and if I get them wrong I want to apologize to the slide-rule boys beforehand.

The word that best describes my impression of what generates high clubhead speed is leverage.

You may remember in history class seeing pictures of what must have been the original form of artillery—a sort of sling affair made by bending a tree over until its top end touched the ground, then securing it with a rope. A stone or some sort of missile would be lodged at the business end of the apparatus and then, when the rope was cut—Whoooosh!—somebody was in for a headache.

To me, the action of that tree represents pretty closely the kind of leverage by which a golfer can most effectively generate clubhead speed. Picture it in your mind's eye. The bending of the tree down to the ground creates a gradual buildup of massive energy—the backswing. The cutting of the rope represents the initial release of pent-up energy—the transition from backswing to forward swing. As it springs back, the tree forcefully but smoothly accelerates, but it retains its maximum release of energy until the last split second—the delayed uncocking of the wrists. There is a final explosive release of energy as the tree whips back to its original position and slings the stone into the

Stored energy, released, is the secret of leverage in the golf swing, much as the tree can be a catapult.

enemy camp—the whipping or slinging of the clubhead through the ball. I can take the analogy even farther in terms of my own game because, at the end of a full drive, I've expended so much energy that I have to make a recoil action—just as the tree would rebound after firing its missile.

At this point I'd rather not get into the technicalities of how I achieve this kind of leverage, except to say that it requires extensive and conscious use of my legs and body, but only passive and virtually unconscious use of my hands and arms. There are two reasons for this. First, I comprehend, without knowing the precise technicalities involved, how clubhead speed derives ultimately from centrifugal force—the force that pulls an object outward from its center of rotation. In my experience, much greater centrifugal force can be developed when the legs and body lever the club than when the hands and arms supply the preponderance of leverage. Second, I have large, strong legs and a fairly powerful torso but rather small, weak hands and arms. Obviously I want to swing in a way that maximizes my strengths and minimizes my weaknesses.

Thus I belong very definitely to the "legs and body" school of golfing thought rather than to the "hands and arms" club. Possibly, if I were differently endowed physically I'd play differently. As it is, to me the legs and body are the engine of the golf swing; they fuel and drive it. The arms are simply connecting rods to the club. I regard the hands as linkage; hinges through which power, first as leverage and then as centrifugal force, is transmitted to the clubhead.

But a warning: This is *my* way. It does not disqualify the fact that some excellent golf has been played with the accent on hands and arms—viz. by Arnold Palmer. If you get your best results by stressing these components, I wouldn't want to be responsible for your changing.

CHAPTER 6

Golf's One Unarguable, Universal Fundamental

The next time you are looking for something to watch on the practice tee at a PGA tour event, study the players' heads as they swing. You'll see a few that swivel—mine included (and I go into that in detail on page 104). But I'd be very surprised if you see many that move up, down, or from side to side.

I regard keeping the head very steady, if not absolutely stock still, throughout the swing as *the* bedrock fundamental of golf. It is inviolable as far as I'm concerned, which is why I bring the subject up this early in the book. If you are hoping to improve your game through these pages, but can't, or won't, learn to keep your head steady throughout the swing, read no farther. There is nothing that I—or anyone else—can do for your golf game.

The reasons the head must stay steady are so obvious to me that I feel a little foolish enumerating them. But since so many handicap players do seem to move their heads around with cavalier abandon, I suppose I'd better. They are as follows:

1. The head, or at least the neck or the top of the spine, is the fulcrum or hub or axis of the swing. As such, any shifting of it up, down, or sideways must inhibit or weaken the springlike coiling of the body on the backswing that is so essential to the generation of proper leverage on the forward swing.

HISTORY'S "QUIET" HEADS

A steady head has certainly been fundamental to the game's finest players. In this century, Walter Hagen would appear to be (I never saw him play) the only superstar who moved his head around during the swing. Personally, I tend to think that this and other swing peculiarities of Hagen's, along with some of his off-course activities, have been exaggerated through the exuberance of the story-tellers. But if it's true he moved his head a lot, it probably explains why he missed so many full shots. Certainly no other twentieth-century champion has been a head-mover. In fact, in one—Arnold Palmer—I believe a "quiet" head has been a premier success factor. With his type of violent swing, I think Arnold's superstill head has often saved his game.

2. Any shifting of the head, at any point from address to impact, will alter the arc and plane of the swing, which, if not a totally destructive factor, is certainly a very complicating one.

3. Movement of the head changes the line of vision, and it tends to force the eyes to alter their image or focus. It is very difficult to hit any object you are not looking at.

4. As the heaviest part of the body, relative to its size, the head has a strong influence on balance. Few people are agile enough to retain their full balance during the exertion of a full golf swing if their head moves.

When you think about these factors it is easy to see why a steady head is the one fundamental of golf that is universal to all "methods" and to all teaching systems throughout history. Hitting the ball as hard as I do, I know I couldn't break 80 if I were unable to keep my head in one place throughout the swing.

That capability did not come easily to me. I believe that keeping the head still is one of the most difficult things a golfer has to learn to do. Certainly it was for me, probably because, in striving for distance through a big arc, it was so easy to sway the top of my body off the ball.

I've told the story before of how Jack Grout finally cured me of head

A simple and effective way to learn to swing around a steady head. If the pupil is slow to respond, the teacher can accelerate his progress by grabbing a handful of his hair—as mine did frequently at one period of my schooling!

movement. When nothing else would work he had his assistant, Larry Glosser, stand in front of me and grab my hair while I hit shots. My scalp still tingles at the thought of those sessions. I cried tears of pain many a time. But by the time I was thirteen I had learned to keep my head in one place, no matter how hard I tried to hit the ball.

Grout is the least sadistic man you'd ever meet, and this was, of course, a last resort. A less-painful technique of his to get a pupil to keep his head still is one I used in hitting thousands of shots as a kid, and still use today to check myself out periodically. Grout applied this technique because he believed a golfer couldn't keep his head steady if he didn't stay well balanced throughout the swing. He felt the key to balance was footwork, and the later success of what he taught me obliges me to agree with him 1000 percent.

Before I was ever allowed to hit woods, Grout made me hit thousands of iron shots—usually with a five-iron—with a flat-footed swing. He made me first plant my heels solidly on the ground, then, during the swing, I was allowed to roll my ankles: the left in toward the right on the backswing and the right in toward the left on the forward swing. But I was not permitted to lift either heel off the ground so much as the thickness of this page.

One invaluable benefit of this exercise was the sound, repetitive pattern of footwork it taught me. Rolling rather than lifting the feet is still integral to my game today. But the main objective originally was to keep me centered and balanced over the ball, and it certainly worked, especially when combined with the hair-grabbing act. Unless you have a tough scalp, I recommend swinging without lifting your heels as the finest of all head-steadying exercises.

The commonest kind of head movement I see among amateurs is lateral. The head shifts away from the target with the club on the backswing then stays there, usually causing the player either to fall onto his back foot and spin his body into the forward swing or, less frequently, to jerk his head forward as the club starts down in a vain attempt to regain his original head position.

Probably the biggest cause of the original fault—the lateral backswing sway—is sheer laziness. Swaying is a cheap way to get the club back and up without turning and coiling the torso; without really stretching and working

STOP HEAD BOBBING

Handicap players often bob their heads up and down during the swing. This is just as fatal, in terms of disrupting the "geometry" of the swing, as lateral movement, but is often even tougher to cure because the movement is usually more difficult for the player himself to detect. As does swaying, I believe bobbing stems mostly from laziness; from making the backswing a lifting action instead of a turning and coiling movement.

A good drill is to get someone to stand in front of you and lay the grip end of a driver lightly on top of your head until you develop the "feel" of a level-headed swing. It might take a while, but it will pay pretty big dividends in the long run.

Many tour professionals swivel the chin away from the target on the backswing, but seldom do they shift it sideways or upward. The sheer momentum of his downswing often causes the good golfer's head to move slightly backward, and sometimes a little downward, through impact and beyond. Such movements are tolerable, so long as they are slight enough to allow the neck or top of the spine to continue to serve as a fixed swing axis.

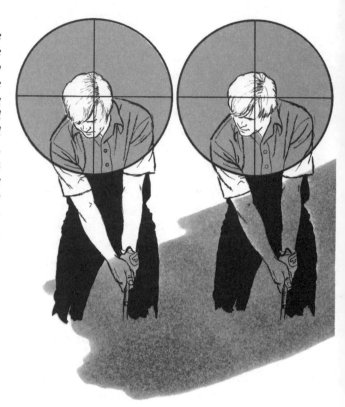

the back and leg muscles. Thus, if you can improve your body pivot going back, there's a good chance that that will automatically take care of your head movement. If not, the only answer is to consciously practice keeping your head steady, *behind the ball,* until it becomes an ingrained habit. To do so, obviously it helps to "keep your eye on the ball." But be wary of that old golfing maxim as head-steadying medicine. I can sway my head two feet and still "keep my eye on the ball."

A final warning: I've been talking all along about a *steady* head, not a stiff or rigid one. The forward sliding of the legs on the downswing can cause a slight lowering and/or backward movement of the head on the forward swing. Such movements are always slight among good players, and are better

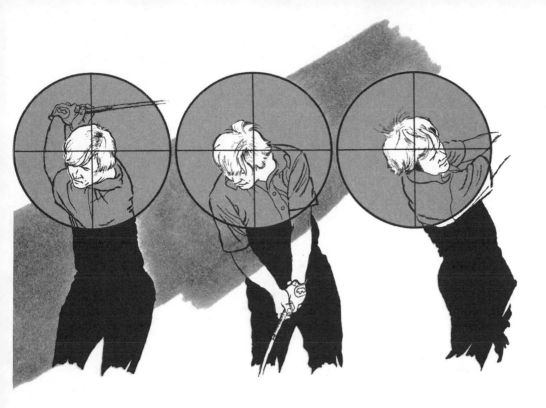

not made at all. But if you find such a slight movement hard to eliminate completely, don't force it. The forward and upward head movement is the one you have to worry about most on your forward swing.

Even in trying to eliminate that, however, you should use your common sense. There must obviously be a pulling-up force on your head as the club rises after impact, and a too-conscious determination to prevent it happening can inject tension or rigidity into your forward swing. The trick is to let the head swivel and rise only when the natural momentum of the through-swing forces it to do so. I find in my own game that this happens automatically if I keep my eyes focused on the ball's original position until the club reaches full extension away from me toward the target.

CHAPTER 7

My Equipment—and Yours

Few club golfers have the time, knowledge, financial ability, inspiration, or desire to get as deeply embroiled in the technicalities of golf clubs as do many of the men and women who earn a living by playing the game. Nor, as I see it, will being hyper-conscious of the finer points of equipment do a great deal for the average twice-a-week golfer's shot-making capability.

I am fairly close to club design through my long and close associations with the MacGregor company. From this relationship, plus my own experiences as a youngster learning the game, I believe that a well-made set of standard modern clubs will suit just about 95 percent of all golfers. The remaining 5 percent are either people to whom some modification might be helpful because of an idiosyncracy of physique or physical condition, or players who've reached so high a level of skill that their only road to further improvement is through very fine tuning. In both those cases, there's a possibility that made-to-measure clubs would help, particularly in building consistency.

The effectiveness of a golf club usually results much more from its influence on a player's mind than on his actual swing. For example, when I'm on my game I can take clubs that are close to those I regularly use and, after a few acclimatizing shots, make them work equally well. In fact, I do just that every time I go to Europe or Australia. I simply adjust my swing fractionally to suit the "feel" and balance of the new clubs that I must use under the terms of my contracts in various parts of the world. Unless he's picked himself a bag of real lemons, the average player could easily make the same adjustment. After a month of regular play with a new set, I'd bet he couldn't tell the difference in "feel" between the new clubs and his old ones. Yet, if his game

USE YOUR INGENUITY

It isn't necessarily true that you'll play best with clubs perfectly uniform in design, shaft flex, and weight (or swing weight). "Matched" sets are a modern invention. Bob Jones won thirteen major championships with clubs acquired one by one from all over the United States and Great Britain. Jim Jamieson tied for second in the 1972 Masters with as miscellaneous a grab bag of sticks as you'll ever see—including a dime-store putter. Many tour professionals use nonmatching drivers, fairway woods, long irons, wedges. The soundest principle is that if it works, use it, whatever its specification.

My Ohio State golf coach, Bob Kepler, followed this principle in a really novel way. He figured that the longer the shot, the more important distance and height became. Thus, in his two- and three-irons he used an A or whippy shaft, the "soft" action of which helped to get the ball up; in his four-, five-, and six-irons a regular R shaft; and in his seven-, eight-, and nine-irons and wedges, where clubface loft guaranteed height, a stiff S shaft. I believe there is a lot in that idea that might help handicap golfers.

improved, I'd bet the new sticks had less to do with his lower scores than did the fact that, to get used to them, he practiced or played more!

I'm not an equipment nut, in the sense of always fiddling around with clubs. You'll rarely see a club lying around my home, unless it belongs to one of my sons, Jackie or Steve. I have a rack full of clubs at my offices, but they're merely spares. A while ago I did buy a sort of do-it-yourself machine shop, but it's still in crates in the garage. One reason I've not assembled it is that we don't yet have three-phase power where I live, but probably a better reason is that I find too many other things to do with my time. For instance, I know I'd certainly much prefer to work on plans for a new golf course than mess around with a driver.

To me, however, there *are* four very important factors in a golf club that all serious players should understand. They are angle of lie; direction of club facing when the club is correctly soled; grip thickness; and the dynamic behavior, or over-all "feel," of the club when swung, which is a product of the interaction of shaft flex and head weight.

Lie—the angle between the head of the club and its hosel—is a critically important factor, much neglected even by good players. If the lie is such that at address the club rests on its toe or heel, rather than flat on its sole, it will meet the ball that way at impact, unless some compensation—a needless complexity—has been made in the swing. Either situation tends to diminish clubhead speed; but worse still is the effect of toe-down or heel-down contact on shot direction. If the toe catches the ground first, the effect will decelerate this section of the club and thus open the clubface through the ball. Conversely, if the heel touches and decelerates first, the clubface will tend to close through the ball. Thus the golfer who fails to sole his clubs flat on the ground at address is inviting loss both of distance and accuracy.

Lie is closely related to a golfer's build and the kind of address posture he adopts. As a rule of thumb, the tall golfer who necessarily stands close to the ball requires a lesser angle between clubhead and hosel—a more "upright" lie—than the shorter golfer who stands farther away from the ball. But address posture must be taken into account, too. I am fairly tall—5 feet 11½ inches—and I set my hands fairly close to my body (this goes with my upright swing plane, but it stems also from my feeling that the farther away the ball is, the more difficult it is to hit). Thus, for my clubs to sole correctly at address, they must lie a couple of degrees more upright than standard. Another golfer my height who stood farther from the ball and tended to hold his hands lower than I do would probably need a slightly flatter lie to achieve perfect soling at address.

IF YOU SLICE, CONSIDER THINNER GRIPS

The size of your hands and what feels most secure and comfortable to you should determine the size of your grips. As a guideline in shot-making terms, I'd say that if you hook the ball, a thicker grip might enable you to hold the club more in your left palm, which has the effect of slowing down the closing of the clubface. Conversely, if you slice, a thinner grip might help you by encouraging more of a finger grip in the left hand, and thus a faster or freer release of the clubhead.

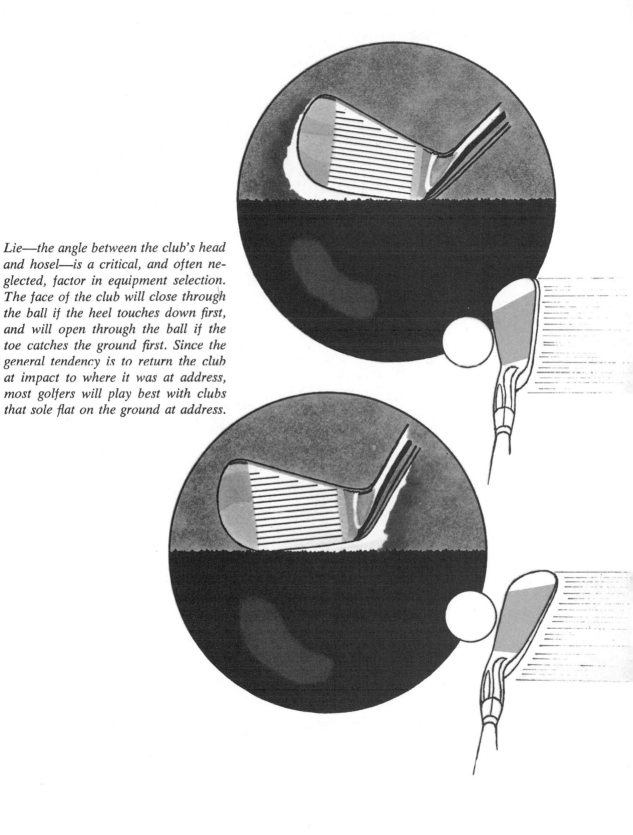

Lie—the angle between the club's head and hosel—is a critical, and often neglected, factor in equipment selection. The face of the club will close through the ball if the heel touches down first, and will open through the ball if the toe catches the ground first. Since the general tendency is to return the club at impact to where it was at address, most golfers will play best with clubs that sole flat on the ground at address.

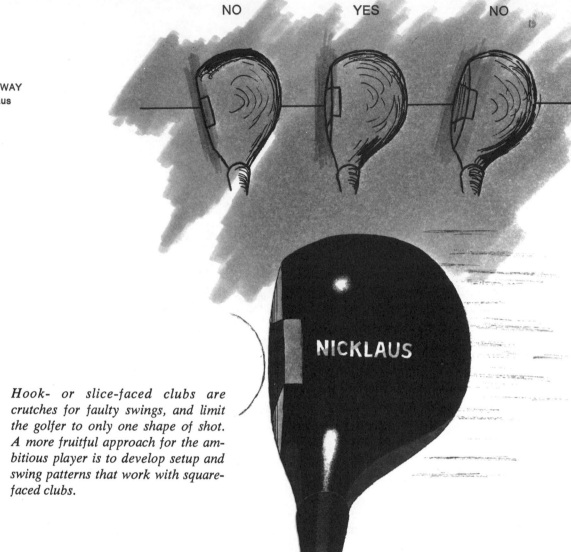

Hook- or slice-faced clubs are crutches for faulty swings, and limit the golfer to only one shape of shot. A more fruitful approach for the ambitious player is to develop setup and swing patterns that work with square-faced clubs.

Your club professional should be able to advise you on lie and if you need any adjustment in your irons, he possibly might be able to make it for you in his workshop. I'm afraid changes in the lie of woods need factory attention. Hopefully you will find a stock set to suit; "standard" lie does vary from manufacturer to manufacturer.

When soled correctly, all my clubs face straight ahead square to my target line, with no "built-in" hooks or slices. I've never cared for a built-in clubface compensation, because in my experience there is a strong tendency to return the clubface square to the target line at impact wherever it looks at address. If it looks left or right of this line at address, to square it by impact usually requires some manipulation of the hands, either early in the backswing or coming into the hitting area. Frequently that instinctive adjustment will be overdone—too much opening or too much closing. This destroys the effect of the built-in clubface misalignment, and you're back to square one: The hook-faced club is opened and you still slice; the slice-faced club is closed and you still hook.

Grip thickness is another important factor often overlooked, again even by the good golfer. Holding the club in a specific, unchanging manner is obviously vital for consistent golf. Either the size of his hands or the kind of linkage "feel" a golfer favors, or both, may necessitate modifications from the standard-grip diameter.

For most of my career I favored slightly oversize grips (one-sixteenth inch thicker than standard), even though my hands are small. I used to set the club very much into the palm of my left hand, because it gave me a nice strong, glued-to-the-club feeling. But that was when I played almost all shots from left to right. As I've learned in recent years to shape shots in both directions, my left-hand grip has changed slightly. The club now sits a little more in the fingers of my left hand (although still basically in my palm), no doubt to allow a slightly earlier closing of the clubface when I want to move the ball right to left.

Related to this is the fact that I've always used leather grips—I just like the feel of leather better than rubber or composition. In the past, by the time I came to renew these grips, I'd often have the feeling that they had gotten thinner—had compressed through usage back down to about standard diameter. Consequently, not very long ago I decided to leave them that way. I now start out with standard-grip thicknesses, and, of course, have my clubs re-gripped as soon as the leather seems to have compressed to a smaller diameter.

This, of course, is personal preference, and I don't think it should influence your decision regarding grip diameter. But the matter may be worth some experimentation on your part.

Incidentally, I find that a left-hand golf glove improves my feeling of grip security, and also saves my hand over intensive periods of practice and play.

When we come to the characteristics of clubs that determine their dynamic behavior during the swing—more simply, their "feel"—we get into a whole maze of variables that, as in so many areas of golf, defy specific analysis. You have to discover what you like and what works best for you *personally*. The only infallible way to do this is by trial and error.

For example, many of the stronger golfers out on tour do not like to "feel the clubhead." In selecting and modifying clubs—a major off-course occupation of many tour pros—they seek a high degree of over-all stiffness or rigidity. They want to feel that the entire club is one solid unit with no sensation of the clubhead bouncing or waving around due to a pronounced

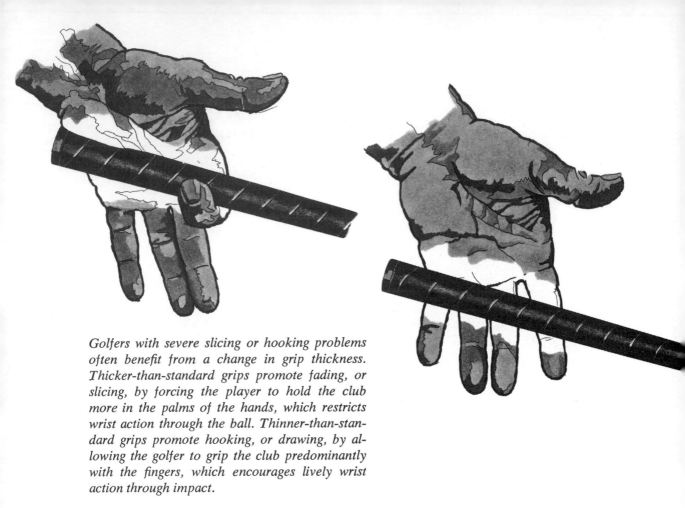

Golfers with severe slicing or hooking problems often benefit from a change in grip thickness. Thicker-than-standard grips promote fading, or slicing, by forcing the player to hold the club more in the palms of the hands, which restricts wrist action through the ball. Thinner-than-standard grips promote hooking, or drawing, by allowing the golfer to grip the club predominantly with the fingers, which encourages lively wrist action through impact.

flexing of the shaft. This desire for stiffness presupposes strength in the player, or at least the ability to create high clubhead speed without help from any flexing action of the club itself. Such a golfer invariably needs control more than distance, and he achieves it by using relatively inflexible shafts with relatively light heads. (The whippier the shaft and heavier the head, the more the club will flex during the swing.) Give a powerful golfer clubs with even slightly softer shafts and heavier heads than his own, and he may hit the ball farther but it will almost certainly take him days to find a way to keep it in the park—if he ever can.

At the other end of the scale are the lady golfer and the lightly muscled or out-of-condition man. Although a stiffer club might feel nice and "light" to such golfers, they often lack the physical capability to swing its business end fast enough to hit the ball the maximum distance they could achieve, even though they might hit it straight.

Thus, such golfers usually benefit from clubs that, through some built-in energy source of their own, reinforce their limited ability to generate clubhead speed. Such an additional energy source can be built into a club by increasing

LONGER CLUBS FOR SHORTER GOLFERS

It seems to me that if anyone is going to benefit from clubs longer than standard, it will be the short, not the tall, golfer. The tall fellow already has an arc big enough to generate good distance. By further lengthening it he may sacrifice accuracy. The small fellow, on the other hand, may find that a bigger arc resulting from a longer club will bring him more distance. Gary Player, who's 5 feet 7 inches, is an example in that his shafts are an inch longer than standard.

If you go to longer clubs, however, remember that you'll need a stiffer shaft to retain the same kind of swing feel that you got with the shorter ones.

its flex to a point where the performance of the shaft itself helps to generate clubhead speed through impact—given, in every case, correct timing of the swing. As a rule of thumb, the stiff shaft performs best for the hard swinger and the flexible shaft performs best for the soft swinger. The old "buggy whip" golf club was the supreme example of the soft-shafted approach. If you could only swing it slowly enough and also perfectly time the arrival of the head at the ball—which few could—you could hit it a hundred miles.

Between the buggy-whip-type action and the telephone-pole-type effect of the XX-shafted clubs used by some very powerful professionals, an infinity of options exists. I believe that the regular clubs currently offered by most manufacturers—average in both shaft flex and head weight—represent about the center point in all these options. The characteristics of most "regular" clubs have been developed through vast searching for a way to meet the average golfers' needs, and I have to believe the result is now pretty well suited to the majority of people.

My own preference is not as far from this center point as you might think, in view of what people like to call my "power game." I've never tried the "buggy whip," but I did experiment with the "telephone pole" for quite a while in 1962. I dropped it after realizing something I should have known all along: Extremes never work for long.

Shafts are normally graded A for whippy, R for regular, S for stiff, X for extra-stiff, and XX for extra-extra-stiff. (Some companies—MacGregor is one—use numerals in place of letters.) From very early in my career I had used S, or moderately stiff, shafts. As an amateur in my late teens and early twenties, my clubs swing-weighted at about D5 to D6. (Swing weight is a concept relating the weight of the grip end of the club to its head weight, in an effort to produce uniform feel in sets of clubs, despite their differences in length and dead weight. The higher the swing-weight designation, the heavier the clubhead will feel in relation to the grip end of the club. Frequently, also, the higher the swing weight, the heavier the club's over-all or dead weight.)

A few years ago it was fatigue at the end of playing thirty-six holes of competition in a day—in the Ryder Cup matches—that made me decide to lose some body weight. Well, it was fatigue years before that caused me to decrease the swinging weight of my clubs. On both occasions the tiredness led eventually to a stronger golf game.

There is a lot of thirty-six-holes-a-day play in serious amateur golf, and eventually I discovered I just couldn't play D6 clubs—especially the driver—for seven or eight hours and still swing them well. Consequently, through experimentation I reduced the swing-weight of my driver to D1. To do so without changing shafts I had, of course, to reduce the club's head weight, and for a while this posed problems, in that—at least until I got tired—I would swing too fast. Gradually, however, I was able to cure this by developing a driver weighing 13.9 ounces, containing an S shaft, and still swing-weighting at D1.

This is the driver formula I reverted to after my best-forgotten "telephone pole" phase of 1962, and it is the one I still use today (although currently, because of a modification described later in this chapter, the club swing-weights at D3). It gives me a firm connection between the clubhead and my hands, while still enabling me to "feel" the clubhead throughout the swing; to know where it is and what it is doing at any point in the action. It represents a club with which I can swing hard and yet still maintain good tempo (the "telephone pole" tempted me to swing harder and thus disrupted my tempo).

My other clubs, excepting the sand wedge, all contain regular (carbon) steel S shafts and swing-weight from D2 to D4, thus producing much the same dynamic effect as the driver—firmness yet enough clubhead feel to promote my ideal swing tempo. The only possibly unorthodox factor about any of the clubs in my bag is that the driver, at 42¾ inches, is a quarter inch shorter than standard. This modification costs me a few yards, but it presents me with exactly the right amount of shaft flex that I feel I need to retain my ideal swing tempo.

The sand wedge I am currently using is an old one I just happened to like when I ran across it one day. It represents a change in attitude from my pre-

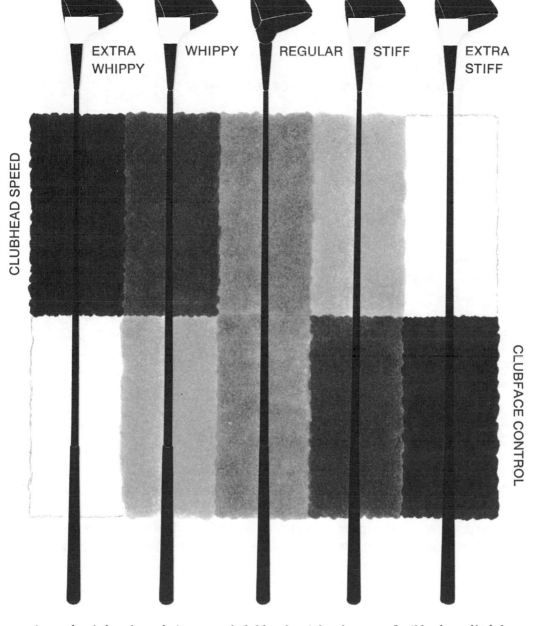

As a rule of thumb, and given equal clubhead weight, the more flexible the golf club
shaft, the more it will help generate clubhead speed; the stiffer the shaft, the more
it will help to deliver the clubface to the ball accurately. Thus, finding the "perfect"
set of golf clubs involves making a compromise between power and control. This is
best done through experience or experiment over a period of time. To generalize,
for those in a hurry, slow "easy" swingers who strike the ball squarely might increase their distance by using more flexible shafts, so long as they can continue to
deliver the clubface to the ball accurately. Conversely, hard, powerful hitters might
increase their control by using stiffer shafts, so long as they do not try to make up
any loss of distance by swinging even harder. The "R," or "regular"-shafted club
(center in illustration), represents the ideal compromise for most golfers.

ASSETS AND LIABILITIES OF THE ONE-IRON

The one-iron requires a well-formed swing and a lot of confidence, but it's a fabulous club for the competent player. It's an excellent driving club on tight holes, and possibly useful for anyone who is wild with fairway woods. I find I get about the same distance from the one-iron as I would from a four-wood, but a lower flight and a longer carry against the wind—and more backspin for greater stopping power. The time to forget the one-iron is from a tight lie or when you're having troubles with long irons generally. (I have more to say about the one-iron under "Power.")

For the beginner or high-handicap golfer, I would suggest the four-wood in place of the two-iron, and the five-wood in place of the three-iron. The five-wood, particularly, is a useful club in that its small head and rounded base enable it to cut through rough and dig balls out of depressions better than any long iron.

vious thinking about pitching clubs. In earlier writings I have mentioned using X or extra-stiff shafts in these clubs because, where distance was no factor, I felt that a stronger shaft increased my control. Now—without really being able to explain why—I've done a complete about-face. Today I prefer a fairly "soft" feel in the wedges; I've simply come to like a "soft" feel through the ball on many of the little shots.

Another reason I like my present, soft-shafted sand wedge so much is that it has only a moderately deep or protruding bottom flange, which makes it a fine pitching club from grass. In one sense this club doesn't really have enough "bounce" for some types of sand—it cuts into fine sand too readily. But on the credit side, the protruding leading edge does get well under the ball. Unfortunately, on the debit side, from a tight lie on grass this same cutting-in action forces me to be wary of hitting fat or gouging in too deeply.

But you can't have it all ways, not unless they bring in a fifteen-club rule. One answer might be to carry three wedges, as Gary Player sometimes does: one for sand alone, one for fairway play, and one for those little pitch shots from grass around the green. Unfortunately, that would cost me too dearly by forcing me to leave out some other club. So I compromise with a fairway wedge, and a combination sand-and-grass pitching club—and the hope that I won't get in sand too often!

Besides my driver and these wedges, the rest of the clubs in my bag are a three-wood, irons one through nine, and a putter that I've been using more or less regularly for ten years. All are of standard length, and there's nothing remarkable or unusual about them, except that—if I may be allowed a small commercial—they are extremely well-designed and made by the MacGregor company, whose products I have used throughout my career.

One experiment I did make a while back was to put a one-ounce plug of lead in the handle of my driver under the grip. The idea was to slow down my hands—improve my tempo by putting more weight in my hands and thus, in effect, less in the clubhead. I believe that this little-known device is helpful when your hands begin to get too fast, either on the takeaway or from the top of the swing. In fact, its effectiveness causes me to question whether the major benefit claimed for aluminum and lightweight steel shafts—that they allow a

BALL COMPRESSION

I use high-compression balls (100) summer and winter. I may not get as much distance in the winter as I could with a lower-compression ball, but I don't want to have to adjust to different impact feels, trajectories, and so on.

I'm told the higher a ball's compression, the farther any golfer will hit it. This may be provable in scientific terms, but I think it's nonsense in human terms. I believe you have to hit a high-compression ball very hard indeed to get the best from it. Apart from that, the stonelike impact feeling of a high-compression ball can be a major psychological deterrent to a naturally soft swinger.

Many tour players use the 90-compression ball because they favor its impact feel, click, and trajectory characteristics over any slight extra distance a higher-compression ball would give them. You should find the compression of ball that pleases you most in psychological terms and stick with it, even if it occasionally costs you a few yards.

heavier head without increasing the club's total weight—is totally valid. You may be able to move the head of such a club faster through the ball, but you've still got to be able to control its other end with your hands. To do that, it seems to me you need a certain amount of weight in your hands.

There's a fishing analogy that both explains what I'm getting at here and makes the basic point about fitting golf clubs to golfers. Suppose you took a very light rod and stuck a heavy weight on the line. To cast any distance you'd really have to "wait" for the rod. You'd have to swing it pretty darn slowly to get the best from its flex action; your timing would have to be right on the nose to put the bait way out there among the fish every time. Now put a series of progressively lighter weights on the line. The lighter the weight, the faster you can swing the rod, and timing becomes less critical to achieving good distance. Maybe you'll never get quite as far out with the lighter weights as you could with a perfectly timed cast using the heaviest tackle. But it's a safe bet your *average* distance is going to be better with the lighter tackle, simply because it is effective even when slightly mistimed.

If your distance still doesn't satisfy you, you still have another option: a heavier rod. That would increase your leverage by putting more weight into your hands relative to the weight at the end of the line. In that way you might outdistance even your *best* casts with the lighter tackle. And, again, it more than likely would increase your control.

Both in fishing and in golf, once you have developed a sound repeating swing, there is a specific relationship of rod or shaft strength to tackle or club-head weight that will help you to cast or hit closest to your best most consistently. In both sports, of course, direction is as important as distance. Thus your ideal equipment must always represent a compromise between power and control.

My golfing compromise, after twenty years of experimentation, is the S shaft combined with a head weight that produces a D1 to D3 swing weight. In fishing terms . . . well, maybe in another twenty years I'll write a book on *that*.

PART TWO

Down the Fairway

CHAPTER 1

The Grip:
Not a Knotty Problem

I have never tied myself in knots concerning the way I hold the club. As I said earlier, the function of my hands and wrists during the swing is simply that of a hinge. I do not hit the ball *with* my hands, but *through* them, using them—unconsciously—to translate body leverage into clubhead speed.

Thus I am concerned with only four factors in gripping the club:

1. That my hands are placed on the club so that more often than not they will *naturally*—unconsciously—deliver its face square to the target at impact.
2. That my hands will accept the shock of impact without slipping on the club.
3. That my hands are linked to the club in a way that allows the wrists to hinge efficiently at certain points in the swing.
4. That the pressure of my hands on the club makes possible factors 1, 2, and 3.

I can deal with the first point—clubface alignment—very simply. I imagine that someone is holding a club up for me so that its sole is correctly grounded and its face is square to my target. I bend over and move my hands forward without altering the alignment they were in as they hung freely at the end of my arms when I stood erect. I then lay them against the grip, fingers open. By offering my hands to the club thus, the back of my left hand and the palm of my right hand will pretty much face the target. Thereafter all I do is

GOLF MY WAY
Jack Nicklaus

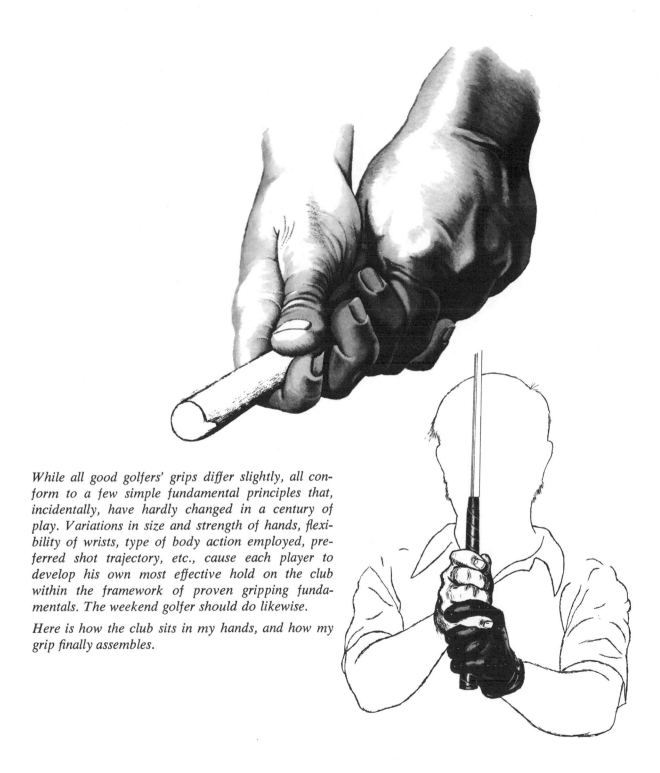

While all good golfers' grips differ slightly, all conform to a few simple fundamental principles that, incidentally, have hardly changed in a century of play. Variations in size and strength of hands, flexibility of wrists, type of body action employed, preferred shot trajectory, etc., cause each player to develop his own most effective hold on the club within the framework of proven gripping fundamentals. The weekend golfer should do likewise.

Here is how the club sits in my hands, and how my grip finally assembles.

TAKE YOUR GRIP WITH CLUB SOLED

When practicing, make a habit of assembling your grip with the club correctly soled and aimed, not while you're waving it around in the air. Firm up the left hand first, with the back of this hand aimed squarely toward the target. Then add the right hand softly enough not to jiggle the clubface out of alignment. Just before you wrap the club into the fingers of your right hand, check that its palm is aimed in the same direction as the back of the left hand—preferably toward the target but, if not, wherever the left hand is facing. If the two don't match, your hands must work in opposition to each other.

wrap the left hand and then the right hand around the club without changing this alignment. The wrapping takes place in such a way that the club lies across both the palm and fingers of the left hand, but predominantly across the roots of the fingers of the right hand. To make the hands as much of a single unit as possible, I also twist a couple of fingers around each other, but we'll get into that later.

That's it for positioning the hands. I believe they function best, in terms of squaring the clubface at impact, when they work instinctively during the swing—when they behave *reflexively* rather than through conscious direction. Instinctively, in hitting just about anything open-handed, your palms will face your target at impact regardless of whatever angles they may pass through as you swing them back and forward. Thus, by setting the palms parallel to the clubface as you set up to swing, you favor both the laws of nature and the laws of reason in achieving a square clubface at impact. To me, it's that simple.

Another factor that's always encouraged me to hold the club with my palms parallel to the clubface—a better way of saying "square to the target"— is the solid resistance to the forces of impact that this type of grip provides. When a club meets a ball at 100 mph or more, some powerful forces are exerted on the hands—especially the leading hand—that can easily cause slippage. Probably the strongest part of the hand is its butt. In fact, I think it was to enable this powerful part of the leading hand to take the blow that olden-day golfers first developed the so-called four-knuckle grip, and is why youngsters

OVERLAP, INTERLOCK, OR TEN-FINGER?

In an experimental mood many years ago I tried both the overlapping and the full-finger grips. I played more than fifty rounds using the overlap, but my hands always felt as though they were coming apart, especially in the impact zone. I gave up the ten-finger grip after much less experiment, because I was never able to make even one full swing with it in which I didn't feel as though my hands were working in different directions. A handful of fine players such as Bob Rosburg and the distinguished British professional, Dai Rees, have used this grip successfully, but it's still not for me.

The overlapping grip—little finger of right hand wrapped around forefinger of left hand—is by far the most popular grip among good golfers, so I guess it should be your first choice. But if it doesn't do as good a "unitizing" job as you'd like, try the interlocking grip. It has served me pretty well.

THE PRESSURE POINTS

I try to hold the club firmly with all my fingers, but there is obviously a stronger sensation of pressure in some than others. In my left hand the last two fingers do a very positive job of hanging onto the club, while wedging it against my palm. In my right hand the thumb and forefinger once seemed to do most of the work, but today I rather think the two middle fingers have adopted the strongest role. But I really do try to avoid relaxing any of my fingers on full shots. I have insufficient strength in my hands and fingers to allow any shirking.

MAINTAIN CONSTANT PRESSURE

I think it's important to try to keep grip pressure constant throughout the swing, even into the follow-through. If you get into the habit of loosening your hands after impact, there's a real danger the habit will creep backward until you're loosening them before impact.

Grip slippage is a guaranteed gamewrecker. Among amateurs the most common point of loosening the hands is the top of the backswing. This forces a regripping of the shaft coming down and is almost certain to alter the clubface alignment. A simple way to check the fault is consciously to nestle the left thumb into the right palm at the summit of your swing, before you change directions.

and frailer golfers today still favor a grip in which the hands are turned well to the right on the club. But to swing the club freely and squarely into the ball with the butt of the left hand leading is, for me, a very difficult maneuver—especially in light of the instinctive tendencies of the hands to return square to the target. Yet the golfer still has to call upon strength in some part of his leading hand to absorb the shock of impact if the club is not to slip as he hits the ball. What's the strongest part of the hand after the butt? To me, it's the *back* of the hand. (To prove this to yourself, just hit something with the back of your fingers, then with the back of the hand itself.) Thus, by having the club very firmly wedged into the palm of my left hand, and by swinging so that the back of my left hand leads into the ball, I minimize the chance of club slippage at impact.

The efficiency of the hinging action of my hands and wrists in transforming leverage into clubhead speed depends on how well they work as a unit. Their working together depends mainly on how closely they can be unified on the club shaft. The baseball player provides a good example of this. When he's going for a home run, distance is all, and he sets his hands as close together on the bat as possible to allow him to generate maximum speed. But when he's called on to bunt, control is everything and distance nothing, so he spreads his hands wide apart on the bat. If you would like to make a little experiment, you'll find it's easy to control the path of a golf club with your hands spread apart on it, but it's one devil of a job to develop much clubhead speed.

The technique I use to mold my hands together as a unit is called the interlocking grip. It involves twining the little finger of my right hand between the index and largest finger of my left hand as I finally assemble my grip. Apart from a short experimental period many years ago, I've used this interlocking method of welding or "unitizing" my hands on all full shots throughout my career. Although the interlocking grip isn't common among good players (see panel, page 71), I believe it is the best hand-"unitizer" going, especially for golfers with small or weak hands.

My grip varies in one other small way from the grips of many tour players. Again, to "unitize" my hands as much as possible, I snuggle the forefinger of my right hand close against its neighbor, and wrap it firmly around the club—no gaps. Many good golfers set the right forefinger on the club in more of a "triggered" position, causing a gap between the forefinger and the club. I believe that the more space the hands take up on the club, the harder it is for them to work as a unit. If only it were practical, the ideal unitizing grip would place the right hand smack on top of the left. (But on reflection, I'm now not sure this is such a terribly significant thing after all, because for a while after I injured my right forefinger in the summer of 1972, I played perfectly well with it hardly on the club at all!)

The final important factor about the grip to me is pressure—how firmly

"LONG" THUMB A GOOD BRACE

Before I modified my left-hand "palm" grip somewhat, I used what the fellows on tour call a "long left thumb." This pushing of the left thumb as far down the shaft as is comfortably possible goes well with a palm grip, especially for the small-handed golfer.

My left thumb is "shorter" now because I hold the club a little more in the fingers of my left hand. Yet I still think a golfer who has trouble hanging onto the club—especially at the top of the backswing—will solidify his grip by laying as much of his left thumb as possible down the shaft.

GOLF MY WAY
Jack Nicklaus

Historically, big hands have been considered an asset in golf, but small ones haven't hindered me (these drawings represent my actual hand size). Perhaps that's because I motivate a golf club primarily with my legs and body, rather than my hands and wrists.

GRIP "WEAK" TO STRENGTHEN SWING

The more to the left of the club a golfer sets his hands, the stronger his swing must be to allow him to draw the ball. The more his grip is turned to the right on the club, the easier it will be to move the ball right to left. I explain this hoping to encourage you to play with what is known as a relatively "weak" grip —palms square to the target—in order to force you to develop a strong swing. You will be a better golfer in the long run than if you use a "strong" grip, with your hands turned more to the right. This grip is a crutch that easily camouflages your swing deficiencies and therefore demands no improvement.

I'm adopting this policy with my eldest son, Jackie. I want him to learn to draw the ball before he learns to fade it—as every beginner should. But I want him to learn to draw with his swing, not his grip.

one grasps the club. Here again I've wavered over the years. I have always believed that the forward hand leads and directs the swing through the ball, and that the following hand "swings the hinge"—transmits the final burst of speed to the clubhead with a last-minute release of the wrists very similiar to that of a baseball pitcher's.

Seeking predominantly to fade the ball most of my career, I adopted—as I've said—very much a palm grip in my left hand. This gave me a distinctly firmer hold on the club in my left hand than in my right. Now, however, as a result of wanting to draw shots more often, my left-hand grip is more in the fingers, and the pressure of both hands on the club is more equal. This allows me to "swing the hinge" with the fingers of my right hand a little faster or earlier whenever I want to curve the ball from right to left.

How firm is the *over-all* pressure of my grip? How tight, or loose, do I hold the club? Frankly, I play so many types of shots today, demanding so many variances in grip pressure, that it is impossible to generalize. But if I had to name a pattern, I'd say I'm of the firm-gripping rather than the relaxed-gripping school. And I'd guess that this is probably true of most "legs and body" players as opposed to "hands and arms" golfers.

CHAPTER 2

Setting Up:
Ninety Percent of Good Shot-Making

I am sometimes accused of being a slow player. Well, the truth is that I walk very fast up to the ball, make a fairly fast decision about what I want to do when I get there, but then sometimes set up to the shot slowly.

There are some good reasons for my being so methodical about my setup. I think it is the single most important maneuver in golf. It is the only aspect of the swing over which you have 100 percent conscious control. If you set up correctly, there's a good chance you'll hit a reasonable shot, even if you make a mediocre swing. If you set up incorrectly, you'll hit a lousy shot even if you make the greatest swing in the world. Every time I try to deny that law by hurrying my setup, my subconscious rears up and beats me around the ears.

In a casual round of golf with friends I can walk up to the ball, put the club down, draw back, and pop it in no time flat. More often than not I'll hit an adequate shot in the sense that it will land somewhere on the fairway or the green. But I cannot play tournament golf that way. Winning in professional golf's present competitive climate demands precise shot-placement on every single hole of every single tournament. For the modern professional golfer to be consistently successful, careful assessement of, and setup to, every shot must become as habitual as eating dinner.

I feel that hitting specific shots—playing the ball to a certain place in a certain way—is 50 percent mental picture, 40 percent setup, and 10 percent

77

HIT FARTHER WITH LESS FUSS

When I want to hit the ball a long way without too much regard for direction—as, for example, on a wide-open par-5 hole—I will often take far less time at address than I normally do.

One reason is that exact alignment isn't so critical; I can aim and fire without being too nitpicky about direction. Another reason I'm quicker off the mark is that, by knowing beforehand such a shot is coming, I build up for it while walking from the last green to the tee by putting myself in a big-hit frame of mind. My objective is to get good and relaxed. Then, once I'm nice and loose, I want to let fly as soon as possible when I stand up to the ball, before any muscular or mental tension can build up.

I often have the same objective on a very long approach putt, where I'm mainly concerned about getting the ball within three or four feet of the hole. I'll try to "feel" the shot generally rather than specifically, then hit it before I lose the "feel," before my stroke can tighten up. One quick glance, and *pop*. But you'll very rarely see me do that on a putt I'm trying to make. Then I need time to concentrate on all the factors of speed and line and grain involved.

swing. That's why setting up takes me so long, why I have to be so deliberate. In competition I am not simply trying to hit a *good* shot, but rather the *perfect* shot for the particular situation. I frequently fail, of course, often because I've mentally pictured the wrong shot. But unless I can set up *exactly right* in relation to the shot I have pictured, I know I have no chance of executing it as planned. Therefore I *must* get perfectly set—it's almost a compulsion—before I can pull the trigger. My mind simply *will not let me* start the swing until I'm "right," no matter how long it takes.

I'd like to emphasize here that I am strongly against slow play, and that I'm conscious I've been regarded as an example of it on tour. Whatever truth there may have been in this at one time, I believe there has been no substance to such an assertion for a long time now. Arnold Palmer made an official complaint about slow play at the U. S. Open at Merion in 1971, apparently directed at me. The following day a number of groups were carefully observed and timed by United States Golf Association officials. Mine was faster than a lot of the others, including Arnold's, despite the fact that my group contained one of the two genuinely slowest golfers on tour! I think today very few of the tour players would accuse me of holding them up when we're paired together—because the fact is that, although I can rarely shorten the time I need to spend setting up to a shot, I now make a deliberate effort to minimize its effect on my playing partners.

I am usually the last golfer in a group to play his fairway shots. At one time, out of courtesy, I would stand by while the others played, then go to my ball and assess my shot while they waited for me. Now, as unobtrusively as possible, I walk ahead to the region of my own ball to make my decisions while the others are playing their shots. So far as is possible I do the same thing on the putting greens. And, if you'd care to notice next time you're at a tournament, I also walk pretty darn fast on the golf course.

The point I'm stressing is the vital importance of the setup on every shot you hit. This includes picturing the shot, aiming and aligning the clubface and your body relative to your target, placing the ball relative to your intended swing arc, assuming your over-all address posture, and mentally and physically conditioning yourself just before pulling the trigger. I think the importance of each of these steps is such that we should discuss them individually.

GOING TO THE MOVIES

I never hit a shot, even in practice, without having a very sharp, in-focus picture of it in my head. It's like a color movie. First I "see" the ball where I want it to finish, nice and white and sitting up high on the bright green grass. Then the scene quickly changes and I "see" the ball going there: its path, trajectory, and shape, even its behavior on landing. Then there's a sort of fade-out, and the next scene shows me making the kind of swing that will turn the previous images into reality. Only at the end of this short, private, Hollywood spectacular do I select a club and step up to the ball.

It may be that handicap golfers also "go to the movies" like this before most of their shots, but somehow I doubt it. Frequently those I play with in pro-ams seem to have the club at the ball and their feet planted before they start "seeing" pictures of the shot in their mind's eye. Maybe even then they see only pictures of the swing, rather than of what it's supposed to achieve. If that's true in your case, then I believe a few moments of movie-making might work some

"Going to the movies" before selecting a club from the bag would make golf a less frustrating game for many weekend players. In my case, visualizing the ball's ultimate resting place forms the opening scene. This is followed by a travelogue in which I imagine how it will get there. The finale in my mind's eye features the setup and swing I'll need to effect a happy ending.

small miracles in your game. Just make sure your movies show a perfect shot. We don't want any horror films of shots flying into sand or water or out of bounds.

AIM AND ALIGNMENT

I've often written in the past that the first action in aiming a shot is to place the club behind the ball with the face square to the target. I still believe this is a good principle for the majority of less-accomplished golfers, for reasons I'll explain. But if you're going to accept it from me, it will have to be on the basis of "do as I say, not as I do."

The fact is that I very rarely square the clubface to my target at address. Usually I set it a little open—aimed slightly to the right of target. I suppose this habit is the result of predominantly fading the ball for so many years. The

open face at impact would naturally cause a fade, but today I often set the club-face a fraction open even when I'm intending to play a draw, then square the face at impact by releasing my hands into the ball sooner. Only when I want to hook, rather than gently draw the ball in from right to left, do I normally align the clubface square to the target at address. Then I give it the same swing I'd normally use to draw the ball from my open-clubface setup.

Some deviation of the clubface from square at address is common among good golfers. I'd guess about half of the players on tour today set the face slightly open at address most of the time, achieving whatever "shape" of shot they desire through some adjustment in swing pattern. Frank Beard, a pronounced right-to-left player—and as natural a swinger of the club as you'll ever see—is a good example of this. The best example I've run across of the other tendency—a closed clubface at address—is the outstanding British tournament professional Neil Coles. At address Coles closes the clubface so much that if he didn't compensate in his swing, he'd hit every shot way left. He also addresses the ball smack in the neck of the club—seemingly guaranteeing a shank with every iron. But the swing pattern Coles has grooved over the years returns the clubface only fractionally closed to the clubhead's path, producing a very powerful draw shot from off the center of the face. Clubface alignment at address, for many accomplished players, may thus be related more to personal swing characteristics and shot-"shaping" objectives than to establishing correct aim and alignment at the start.

I think the lesser player, however, should aim the clubface on-line. The reason is that until he achieves a fairly advanced level of skill, plus an intimate knowledge of golf's basic laws of cause and effect, he will tend instinctively to align *himself* according to where he aims his clubface. An open clubface will cause him to align himself to the right, a closed clubface to the left. In some instances, that may not be all bad. If he also *swings* the way he's aimed and aligned—thus matching the path of the clubhead to the direction of its face—there's a good chance he will hit the ball to his target: either by hooking it in if he aims and sets up right, or by cutting it in if he aims and sets up left. The trouble is that many golfers do not swing that way—at least, not coming down. Instead, on the forward swing they instinctively try to make the path of the club follow the *actual target line*. Instinct forces them to swing down along the target line rather than along the line parallel to their bodily alignment. The result, in the case of the golfer aiming right, is that he works the clubhead back to the ball from outside, or beyond, the target line, usually causing a pull to the left or a pull-slice that starts left and curves right—the opposite of the "shape" he's actually set himself up to hit. In the case of the golfer aiming left, he works the club back to the ball from well inside the line, causing a push to the right or a push-hook that starts right and curves left—again the opposite of his setup shape.

Therefore, certainly until he fully understands golf's basic laws of cause and effect, I believe a golfer generally benefits by aiming the clubface square to the target as his first move in setting up to the ball. Thereby he at least establishes a reliable dimension by which to align his body parallel to his target line. And by paralleling his body to his target line at address, he gives himself the best chance, *instinctively* as well as consciously, of swinging the clubhead along it at impact.

Long-winded as this may sound, proper alignment can be vitally important to a golfer who consistently slices or hooks the ball, and can't figure out why. You cannot evade the effects of the interrelationships of clubface alignment and swing path at impact—either in trying to deliberately "bend" shots or in trying to remove unwanted "bends." Nor, until they achieve a reasonably high level of skill at golf, can most players consistently subdue instinct with reason. Thus it usually pays to start from a base—square clubface and body alignment—where instinct can dictate an on-line clubhead path through impact.

Having taken quite a few words to suggest that the average golfer is best off with a square body alignment at address, I'm now going to tell him that my body is actually aligned very slightly left of target on most shots. Again, this has to be a case of "do as I say, not as I do."

When I began golf I was taught to stand square to the clubface—toes, knees, hips, chest, and shoulders parallel to my target line. I stayed with that setup until I developed enough swing control to determine that, for all the reasons I've explained in previous chapters, I wanted to "block out" the left side of the course by flighting the ball basically from left to right.

SET UP FROM THE LEFT SIDE

I always work myself around into setup position from the left of the target, never from the right. The main reason for this is that, if I can't be perfectly aligned, I'd rather be angled too much left than right. I'd rather "miss" the ball from left to right than from right to left.

A secondary reason is that, for me, hitting or throwing anything becomes easier the more my body faces the target—the more "open" it is at the moment of release. I can return a baseball far more powerfully and accurately from the outfield by throwing from an "open" body position than from a closed one. Tennis is another example. The natural—and thus the easiest—way for me to hit tennis shots is from an "open" body position.

I think it's true to say that all good golfers work into their setup for address from an open-bodied position—in other words, as they step into their stance their left side moves from left to right. I can't remember ever seeing a tour player plant his left foot first when stepping up to the ball. He puts his right foot into position first, while half facing and "sighting" his target. Then he eases his left foot and body into position from the left of the target line.

What I wanted as a bread-and-butter shot was a very slight fade, a shot that flew very slightly left of target at the start, then curved very gently back to it at the end—a far different animal from the "banana balls" that cause all those "Fores!" on Saturday mornings. For the ball to fade as I wanted it to, at impact the club had to be moving very, very marginally across the target line from the outside, and the clubface head to be very *slightly* open to the club's *fractionally* outside-in path.

As a youngster I had found it possible to achieve this impact "geometry" from a square setup, basically by using a lot of leg and hip action and a delayed release of my hands. But in achieving the fade this way, I was, in effect, forcing myself to change horses—or swing arcs—in midstream. I was starting the club-head back along the target line, then returning it fractionally from the outside. Sometimes, when I overused my legs and overdelayed my hands, the fraction turned into a furlong, and I'd hit the mother and father of all slices.

Eventually it dawned on me that there was another and an easier and more reliable way to fade the ball. Why not just set up the shape at address? Why not align my body a little left, open the clubface a degree or two, then make a normal swing on a natural path—the path parallel to my body alignment? All of a sudden swinging the club became easier. I could hit the ball more freely and thus more powerfully. Less frequently did my fade turn into a giant banana. At the same time, of course, I learned that it was much easier to draw the ball by aligning to the right, closing the clubface fractionally, and swinging naturally (parallel to my body line) than by standing square, slowing down my leg action, and speeding up my hands.

For most of my career I established my body alignment at address by relating myself to the clubface. I would find a leaf or some sort of mark on the grass on the target line a few feet ahead of the ball; line up the clubface while looking from behind the ball through my mark to the target; then, holding the clubface in position, sort of walk around it and align myself in an address position square to the face. About three years ago I modified this procedure for two reasons: First, I couldn't hold the clubface steady enough for my liking while I walked around it; second, I found I wasn't actually squaring the clubface to the target, but setting it slightly open.

Today I still find a mark ahead of the ball on my intended line, I still walk around into address from behind the shot, and in my mind's eye I still "see" a line connecting the ball and my mark. But today my line doesn't run to the target as it used to do. Now it is angled as many degrees left or right of the target as I want to fade or draw the ball. You may have noticed that I look along the line from the ball to the mark two or three times as I settle into my

Many golfers fail to execute intentional fade or draw shots as planned because of faulty address alignment rather than actual swing errors. Using my bread-and-butter fade as an example, these drawings illustrate how I aim my clubface and myself to curve the ball to my target. First, I determine the starting line of the shot (represented here by the solid line in the top drawing). To allow myself to swing the club through the ball in that direction, I must align myself at address parallel to that starting line. I do not, as so many golfers do, align parallel to the actual target line (dashed line lower drawing). I do aim my clubface at the actual target, which is right of my starting line, to produce the sidespin necessary to fade the ball back to the target (see right half of lower drawing). I find it helpful to pick out a spot a few feet ahead of the ball, on the shot's starting line, by which to check that my feet and shoulders really do parallel that line and not the true ball–target line.

SWING PATH

SWING PATH

SHOULDER ALIGNMENT GOVERNS PATH OF CLUBHEAD

Whatever alignment you seek at address—open, square, or closed—don't make the mistake of thinking that by aligning your feet one way your body will automatically follow. Every time I play in a pro-am I see golfers with closed stances and open body positions or open feet and closed bodies.

Among tour players, Lee Trevino best exemplifies the fact that foot alignment doesn't automatically govern body alignment. Lee's feet are aligned way left of target on all his full shots but, by the time he's shuffled his body into its final takeoff position, his hips and shoulders usually are aligned only slightly left of target.

The critical alignment factor is the shoulders. Remember that, unless you make a deliberate effort not to, you will instinctively swing the club through the ball parallel to your shoulders, no matter where your feet may be aligned.

address position. What I'm doing is squaring my body—particularly my shoulders—to this mentally visualized line that indicates the ball's starting direction. When I do the job right I know I am correctly set up for whatever shape of shot I plan. Assuming my clubface is correctly matched to the degree of curve I intend, all I have to concentrate on then is swinging the club back and forward along the line between the ball and the mark—in other words, parallel to my body alignment.

BALL POSITION

I play every standard shot with the ball in the same position relative to my feet. That position is opposite my left heel.

Although down through the years many good players have used one ball position for all basic shots—I believe Byron Nelson and Ben Hogan both did—others have preferred to move the ball about in relation to the feet, depending on either the club they were using or the type of shot they intended to play.

Thus, since both systems have worked, there can be no hard-and-fast rule on the matter for golfers in general. But, so far as my own game is concerned, I keep the ball's position fixed, for the following reasons:

First, simplicity is my ultimate objective in the golf swing. I strive hard to eliminate needless complexities from what must, by its very nature, always be a highly complex action. Unless one is forced to do so by angled terrain or the demands of an unorthodox shot, moving the ball's position at address is to me a needless complexity.

Second, in a full, free, powerful golf swing, the clubhead travels along a straight path very momentarily. The talk you sometimes hear about swinging "on line for a foot or more through the ball" is so much bunk. The ideal is to have the clubhead traveling along the correct path with its face correctly aligned during that infinitesimal moment when the ball is actually on its face. In the swing I have developed, all those things concur with every club—all the dimensions are most often right—when the ball is positioned in line with my left heel. If I played the ball back an inch or two and still made a standard swing, the clubhead would meet the ball too soon. It would be traveling from inside my chosen target line, and the face would be looking to the right. My basic shot would then become a top, a push, or a push-slice. Conversely, if I played the ball forward and made my normal swing, the clubhead would meet the ball after it had reached the bottom of its arc, it would be traveling back to the inside of my line, and its face would be closing. I would thus be prone to hit fat, to pull or pull-hook most shots.

The third reason I position the ball in line with my left heel relates to the way I develop leverage in my swing. To generate clubhead speed through leverage I must use my legs and hips forcefully on the forward swing. The effect of this is to move the arc of the downswing forward a little—nearer to the target. Positioning the ball opposite my left heel forces me actively to "move into it" with my legs in order to still catch it just before the clubhead reaches the bottom of its arc. If I positioned the ball back farther, I'd either have to restrict my leg and hip action on the forward swing, or risk topping the ball because the clubhead was descending forward of it.

But let me warn you once again against copying me too closely. Each golfer's ideal ball position, relative to his feet, depends on his individual swing style. As a generalization, it might be safe to say that the "legs and body" player will naturally tend to play the ball fairly well forward, whereas the "hands and arms" player will naturally have it fairly well back in the stance. But even within that general framework, the individual golfer must still experiment to find his own ideal ball position.

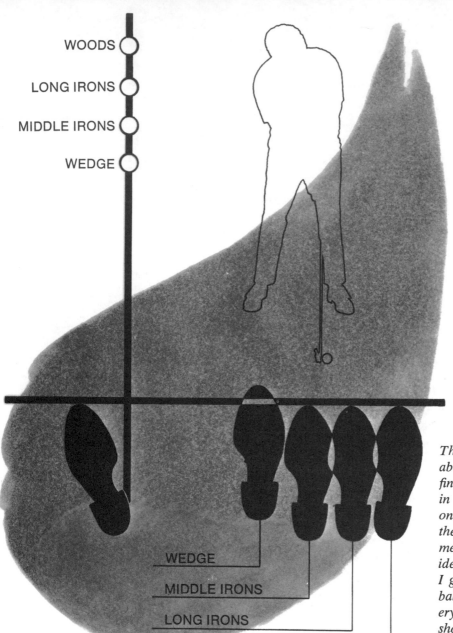

WOODS

LONG IRONS

MIDDLE IRONS

WEDGE

WEDGE

MIDDLE IRONS

LONG IRONS

WOODS

There are two schools of thought about ball position. A number of fine golfers vary the ball's position in relation to the feet, depending on the club being used. However, the trend among modern tournament players is to position the ball identically for every standard shot. I go with the moderns, setting the ball opposite my left heel with every club in the bag for all normal shots.

What about distance of the feet from the ball? Once again there can be no set rule. Much will depend on your height, build, and what feels natural and comfortable. Obviously you should avoid crouching or reaching, and naturalness pays off best, as it does in so many other areas of setup and swing.

I use a simple routine to check that I'm set up at the correct distance from the ball. First, I stand upright but relaxed. Then I flex my knees slightly and relax my shoulders, letting them slump forward and downward. Next I grip the

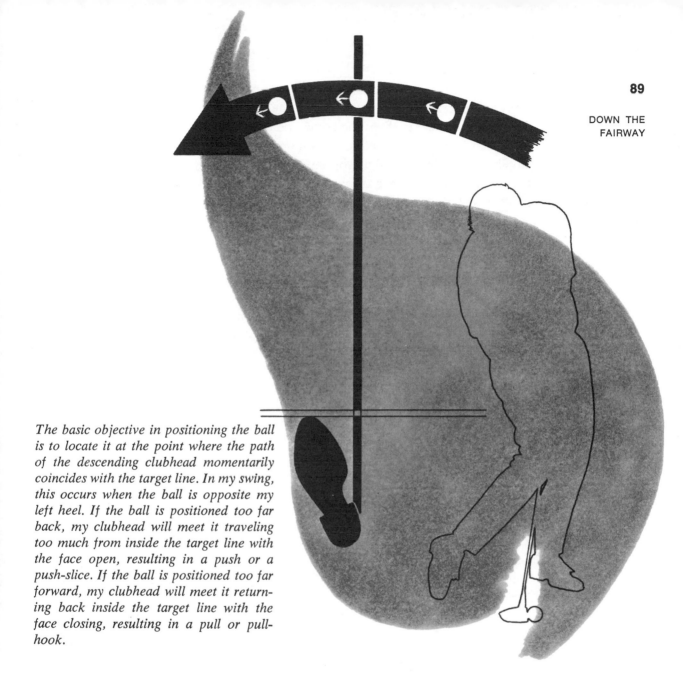

The basic objective in positioning the ball is to locate it at the point where the path of the descending clubhead momentarily coincides with the target line. In my swing, this occurs when the ball is opposite my left heel. If the ball is positioned too far back, my clubhead will meet it traveling too much from inside the target line with the face open, resulting in a push or a push-slice. If the ball is positioned too far forward, my clubhead will meet it returning back inside the target line with the face closing, resulting in a pull or pull-hook.

club and extend it out directly behind the ball, bending just enough at the waist to let my arms hang comfortably with a very slight bend at the elbows. Finally, I ensure that my left arm and club dip only slightly beneath an imaginary straight line running from the top of my left shoulder to the ball.

This maneuver sets me fairly close to the ball, which melds with my upright swing plane and also with my feeling that the ball is easier to hit when it's fairly close to you, so long as you still allow room for your arms to swing past your body. There have been some very fine players who tended to stand well away from the ball. Arnold Palmer is one; and, of course, this goes with his flatter swing plane. Perhaps the critical point to remember about ball positioning is that you want your address position to duplicate your impact position as closely as possible, and that you must be in balance to hit the ball hard and accurately. Overcrowding or overreaching for the ball at address will often be reflected in lack of balance at impact.

ADDRESS POSTURE

My over-all posture at address is determined largely by the factors I've already described: my mental picture of the shot and the body aim or alignment and ball positioning I need to physically execute what I "see."

There are a few detailed points of posture worth looking at, but before we do so let me offer a bit of general advice. Try to avoid getting all knotted up in the way you stand to the ball. First, don't exaggerate anything—"butt out," "hips forward," "chin back," "straight left arm," "low right shoulder," and so on—beyond what feels comfortable. Remember that in your address position you are attempting to mirror your impact position. Anything you do that is forced or contrived or exaggerated at address will almost certainly fall prey to your *instinctive* actions at some point during the actual swing. So try to be as natural as possible within the simple fundamentals of good setup.

The width of the stance and the angling of the feet are closely related postural factors we haven't touched on yet, so let's have a look at them.

I was taught to play, and still do play, from the "insides" of my feet. This was an insurance against losing balance or swaying my head or upper body while hitting the ball hard. I put in many, many hours of exercises—like rocking sideways on my ankles—designed to teach me to stay on the inside of my right foot going back, and on the inside of my left foot coming down. The dividends I've since reaped from these drills make me eternally grateful to Jack Grout for verbally whipping me into performing what was then a very boring regimen.

Playing from the inside edges of the feet requires an equal distribution of weight at address, not only between the two feet, but also between the ball and heel of each foot. On full shots it also requires a fairly wide stance. On more effortless swings the stance can be narrowed without causing the weight to shift to the outsides of the feet.

Thus, with a driver, I adopt a relatively wide stance—about the width of my shoulders between my heels—and gradually narrow it as the clubs shorten

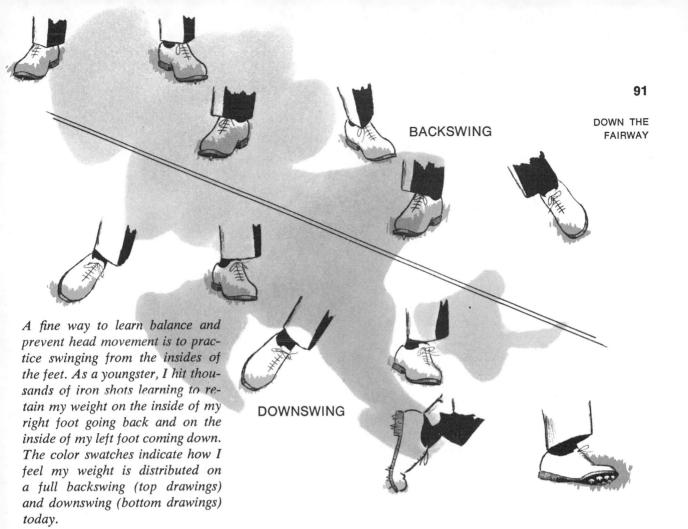

BACKSWING

DOWNSWING

A fine way to learn balance and prevent head movement is to practice swinging from the insides of the feet. As a youngster, I hit thousands of iron shots learning to retain my weight on the inside of my right foot going back and on the inside of my left foot coming down. The color swatches indicate how I feel my weight is distributed on a full backswing (top drawings) and downswing (bottom drawings) today.

and the swing force decreases, to probably only 6 inches with the wedge. I effect this narrowing simply by moving the right foot closer to the left. In that way I maintain a constant relationship of the ball to my left heel. As I narrow my stance, I also "open" it by setting my left foot progressively farther from the target line.

Years of practice and play, plus the fairly athletic life I lead off the golf course—true even when I was a bigger fellow than I am now!—have given me enough suppleness to let me make a very full body turn on the backswing, and a strong leg-hip drive-and-turn on the forward swing from a relatively wide stance. A less supple golfer might find that he needs a narrower stance than mine to facilitate these actions. Then the trick is to find a stance width that permits effective body action without throwing weight to the outsides of the feet or that promotes swaying instead of turning the upper body.

The angling of the feet is also closely related to build and suppleness. On drives I point my right foot just slightly more than 90 degrees away from the

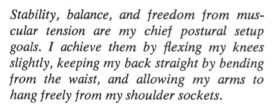

Stability, balance, and freedom from muscular tension are my chief postural setup goals. I achieve them by flexing my knees slightly, keeping my back straight by bending from the waist, and allowing my arms to hang freely from my shoulder sockets.

Striking the ball with the hands slightly ahead of the clubhead is fundamental to solid shot-making. For all normal shots, I establish this impact "geometry" at address. Because my left shoulder is always closer to the target than the ball, I simply set up with my left arm and the club forming a straight line.

target, but place it pretty much at right angles to the target line for most other shots. The purpose of the latter "square" positioning is simply to limit my turn on shots where I don't need full power—it prevents me from moving my hips too far around and thus overswinging. Other golfers may find such an alignment too much of a backswing brake. If so, they might be better off angling the right foot a few degrees farther right, as I do with the driver.

I point my left foot more toward the target—about 30 degrees left of square—on all shots. This toeing out encourages and facilitates fast clearing, or turning out of the way, of my hips after my legs have begun their forward-swing driving action. With the left foot "square" to the target line, it is difficult to clear the hips. Without my pronouncedly "open" left foot placement, I would tend to release the clubhead prematurely and hook a great many shots. But again, the left-foot angle I adopt may not suit a different type of player—especially a "hands and arms" player. Toeing out the left foot also can intensify the already highly developed tendency of many average golfers to swing the right shoulder out and around—instead of down and under—from the top of the backswing. Only intelligent experimentation will teach each individual what's right for him.

Having started with the feet, let's work upward in looking at other postural factors. So next, the knees.

I understand that some of the latest swing "methods" advocate pronounced bending of the knees at address, to "anchor" the golfer's lower half on the backswing and to facilitate a strong leg drive into the forward swing. Maybe that's okay for some people, but for me just a slight flexing of the knees at address works best. Stiff legs are definitely *verboten*—like stiff anything else in golf. But in my case, too much bending of the knees tends to make my leg action saggy and sloppy. I want my legs to be *firmly resilient,* and they become that way with just a slight, natural flexing of the knees at address.

Next, the hands, wrists, and arms.

Most good players and teachers regard leading the clubhead into the ball with the hands as fundamental to solid, accurate shot-making with every club in the bag. If this is so—as it certainly is in my case—and if it is also true that what you are really doing at address is previewing your impact position, then the hands should obviously be set ahead of the ball at address.

My own method of ensuring this positioning is very simple. For any normal shot, I address the ball with my left arm and the club forming a straight line. Even though the ball is positioned fairly well forward, my left shoulder is always closer than the ball is to my target. This forces the straight line formed by my left arm and club always to be angled slightly away from the target. Thus my hands *must* be ahead of the ball. It is an unchanging relationship established automatically by the unbroken arm-club line and the constant ball position opposite my left heel. In fact, it must be fifteen years since I've even had to think about this particular setup factor.

There are other benefits to be derived from setting up with the left arm and club in line. First, this automatically helps establish the correct shoulder tilt at address, with the left shoulder slightly higher than the right, just as it should be during impact. Second, it encourages the right arm to fall into the correct slot, slightly "under" the left, again as is desirable during impact. Third, and perhaps most important, a straight-line relationship between the left arm and shaft at address definitely, in my case, promotes a smooth start to the swing, with everything moving together as a one-piece unit. I think that allowing a concave kink at the back of the left wrist at address will almost certainly cause the hands to work independently by encouraging a dragging back of the club-head, often outside the line. Conversely, a convex arching or forward bowing of the left wrist at address tends to force the hands and wrists independently to lift the club abruptly on the backswing. In either case you're going to be hard-pressed to make a one-piece takeaway.

Finally, the head. I have discussed its very critical role in the golf swing at length in a previous chapter, but to close these thoughts on posture, let's describe where I locate my head at address.

For all normal shots I position my head well behind the ball—where I want it to remain throughout the swing. I also turn my chin slightly away from the target to allow me to look at the ball with my left eye. Just before my take-away I will turn the chin even farther to the right—the movement that actually triggers my swing. But these are mannerisms. The important point is that you set your head *behind* the ball. How far? Well, if you drew a vertical line straight up from the ball, in my case it would connect with my left ear. Only with this positioning can I be sure of delivering the clubhead to the ball with most of my weight behind it. I believe the same holds true for all golfers.

MENTAL AND MUSCULAR CONDITION

The more tense you are at any point in the swing, the more difficult it becomes to hit the ball far and true. Being mentally or physically tense at address is the surest way not to score well.

As I know from almost daily experience, it is very easy to say "don't be tense," but very tough to follow that advice. However I may seem to the fan outside the ropes or watching golf on TV, I do feel pressure. I get nervous, anxious, uptight. It is often as tough a job for me to stay loose over a critical shot as it is for the weekend golfer needing an easy par to win his club's member-guest tournament.

The biggest tension-reliever of all in golf is confidence. If you know exactly what you want to do and have succeeded in doing it sufficient times previously to believe you have an excellent chance of doing it again, you're in good shape. Unfortunately, you can't buy confidence. It's a product of hard-won skill and experience and thus in short supply among play-for-fun golfers.

The second-best tension-reliever, however, is within anyone's capacity. It is concentration: focusing the mind so firmly and so positively on the job at hand as to squeeze out all superfluous and negative thoughts. I am lucky in that I seem to have the gift to concentrate pretty well most of the time on whatever I happen to be doing. But concentration also can be developed and strengthened

LOOKING AT THE BALL

Usually I look at the ball as whole, not at a particular part of it. But I have found on occasions that focusing specifically on the rear half of the ball helps me make better contact.

Although I'm right-handed, I feel my left eye is my master eye. At least, it has become my master eye in golf. It's the one through which I predominantly "see" the ball. This has to be true because, at the top of the swing on a full drive, my head is so positioned that my nose blocks my right eye's view of the ball.

My right eye does have a role, however. Through what I believe is called peripheral vision, I actually see the club start back from the ball. I can—and do—check that it's on the correct path. I feel I do this predominantly with my right eye.

Although I consciously look at the ball until well after impact, I'm never conscious of seeing it hit. It just suddenly vanishes. But even without looking after it, I can tell exactly where it's going from the "feel" of impact.

with training and self-discipline over the years, by almost any player willing to make the effort.

Yet even my concentration can falter. Whenever I am "up" for golf—when either the tournament or the course, or best of all, both, excite and challenge me—I have little trouble concentrating, and therefore little trouble with tension. But whenever the occasion doesn't stimulate or challenge me, or I'm just simply jaded with golf, then is the time I have to bear down on myself with a vengeance. What I suppose I'm really saying is that, in my case, lack of concentration—and thus tension—can result from becoming stale (too much golf in any one short period without sufficient time to rejuvenate) as much as from pressure.

A classic example was the World Series at Firestone in Akron, Ohio, in September of 1972. Life off the golf course for much of that year had been rugged, not only for me but for Barbara and the kids and other members of our family and our close friends. Everybody in the world of sport, except me, seemed to be talking about the "Grand Slam" all year from the first minute of January 1 onward! Even before the Masters in April I seemed to have become the focus of constant attention, the guy in the middle of the merry-go-round. I found this attention unappealing. I like normality. I may want to win more golf

A HELPFUL ANCHORING DEVICE

One little setup aid I find very helpful is a slight inclining or setting-in of the right knee toward the target. This helps anchor my weight on the inside of my right foot while I make a full backswing turn. If I keep this knee in this inclined, slightly flexed position throughout the backswing, I invariably reach the top in position to use my legs properly on the forward swing.

championships than anyone else, but I have no yen for the pomp and circumstance of kingship, especially if it filters into my own home where Barbara and I are trying to bring up five kids who will be just like everybody else's kids.

On top of this I had found myself getting more up and down mentally and physically during the year, even higher for each major championship than in previous years. Losing the British Open obviously caused a major letdown, but I got over that in a few days. What really concerned me as the summer waned was returning to normality, both in my home life and—by this point—also in my career. "It's all very well to want to win major championships," I told myself, "but you're too young a man to be fading off the tour just because of that ambition." And I could see a real danger of that happening.

An infected finger had prevented me from making a full physical preparation for the PGA Championship, so I was unable to get all the way "up" for it. But then came the Westchester Classic. I didn't want to play. I was tired and lacking confidence in my game. I wanted to wrap it up for the year. But I had no valid excuses. Quitting at that point would have been copping out. So I said to myself: "This is it, Nicklaus. Here's a fine tour event on an unusual course, with a big prize. Here's where you've got to get back in the groove. Bear down." Well, it worked: I bore down and I won. Then came the L. & M.-sponsored PGA Match Play Championship at the Country Club of North Carolina in Pinehurst. Again, deep down, I didn't want to play. But, again, while I could conjure up lots of excuses for not competing, none of them contained real iron. And here there *was* a specific challenge: the fact that I'd been eliminated in the first round the previous year. But most of all, it was a big tournament on a fine course, and I was supposed to be a pro. So again I bore down and got "up," and again I won. And in so doing I proved, at least to myself, that I *was* still a pro.

Then, very soon after, came the World Series at Firestone. This event has been extremely kind to me over the years; I have excellent relationships with the sponsors, and I have always wanted to do well in it—who wouldn't, in what is both a TV spectacular and a kind of playoff among the year's top golfers?

At Akron I tried to bear down, but it didn't work. I'd had it. I was burned out. I couldn't force myself to concentrate, and the more I played the more tense I became. The more tense I became the more diabolical the shots I hit, and thus the tension increased even more. It got so bad in the end that it affected not only my own game but, I felt, my opponents' as well. I believe that I have a good relationship with my fellow pros. It's something I cherish and want to keep. But on the sixteenth hole in the second round I began to feel really concerned about my behavior that weekend. Walking down the fairway I just had to apologize to Gary Player and Lee Trevino and Gay Brewer.

"Fellows," I said, "I've been nasty, mean, and irritable, and if I've offended you, I'm sorry. I hope it won't happen again." Thankfully they took it in good spirit, because I'm sure they themselves all know the "down" feeling only too well.

The point I want to make is that whether it's from staleness, as in this instance, or from pressure, as is more often the case, tension does its worst work when you stand up to the ball. A tense mind breeds tense muscles, and tense muscles make you feel clumsy, out of gear. It becomes difficult to aim and align properly; nothing feels right, even when you know everything is correctly positioned. You become "tight," wooden—especially in the hands and forearms,

ELBOW ANGLES

There are numerous schools of thought about the positioning of the elbows at address. Some experts argue that the flat insides of the arms should face out or upward. Some say they should face each other. I've even heard it said the elbows should point down.

I don't go along with any elbow position that's contrived or strained. It seems to me that the insides of the arms should face pretty much at address where they face when they hang naturally at your sides—which in my case is neither upward nor facing, but about halfway between.

ON NOT GROUNDING THE CLUB

I almost always start the swing with the club held slightly above the ground. I think the habit started because I played so many shots as a kid out of Scioto's fescue rough. The ball tends to sit on top of this type of grass, and grounding the club would occasionally cause the ball to roll over. I guess I developed a bit of a phobia about the stroke penalty imposed for moving the ball.

I've stayed with the habit for other reasons, though. First, it prevents stubbing the club going back. Second, it forces me to start back slowly and smoothly. Third, it helps me to break down tension at address. Finally, not being allowed legally to ground my club in a trap is no concern at all.

How close to the ball do I position the clubhead? As close as my nerve permits (which is closer some days than others!). A point I do concentrate on is playing the ball off the center of the clubface. Some good golfers address the ball off the toe or heel of the club and then compensate in the swing, but to me that's a needless complication.

the legs and the upper back. You feel stiff, inflexible, rigid. You can get to a point mentally where swinging the club back correctly begins to seem like a physical impossibility.

In this condition I will play, at worst, disgustingly—I will literally embarrass myself—and, at best, I'll be mediocre. Thus, to bear down as I did at Westchester and Pinehurst in 1972, I must concentrate far more on the preparations for my swing than on the actual swing itself. If I can get the thing set up properly, sheer instinct will usually enable me to make a reasonably good pass at the ball.

How, specifically, do you make yourself bear down? I think the only answer, really, is plain willpower. You just have to force other thoughts aside. You have to discipline yourself vigorously: *make* yourself think exclusively about your aim and alignment and your ball position and your posture; *make* yourself do what you know is right in these areas, and *make* yourself keep on doing it time and time again, even though it doesn't seem to be working. The fact is that if the fundamentals of setup that you are applying are sound, and if you can make yourself stick with them long enough—if you have enough resolution—they *will* ultimately begin to work. And as soon as they do, the tension will begin to evaporate. I've proven this to myself a thousand times in my career, and I'm sure I'll have to go on proving it another thousand times.

For me, getting my mind off tension-producing thoughts becomes easiest when I concentrate on the game itself—especially my setup—rather than its

HOW MANY SWING THOUGHTS?

The time to focus your mind on key swing thoughts is as you settle into your final address position.

When my concentration is good I can focus my attention at address on five or six different things I want to do in the swing, and then actually do most of them. For example, in the 1972 U. S. Open at Pebble Beach, where I was playing many left-to-right shots, at address on any particular shot I might simultaneously be thinking of making a specific type of forward press; keeping my head in a certain position on the backswing; keeping my hands low going back; making a very slow and deliberate takeaway; keeping the back of my left wrist to the target; making a full backswing; working my legs in a particular manner; keeping my head back during the forward swing. When I am not concentrating well, however, I find I can focus attention at address on only one or two swing keys.

How many you can usefully focus on will depend on your levels of skill and concentration. On average, I'd say that two is about the handicap golfer's limit, and that he'd be better off most of the time with only one key swing thought.

I must stress, however, that no matter how many things you think about at address, you are, so to speak, merely programming the computer. Once you throw the switch, the computer must take over. The golf swing happens far too fast for you consciously to direct your muscles. Frequently I can make very minor adjustments in midswing, but they are always instinctive, never conscious.

possible result: winning, losing, making money, or whatever. The more tense I am, the more I try to think of just one shot at a time, one situation at a time, rather than some greater problem—or even area of relief—that might be around the corner. I try to work on the score piece by piece, not as a whole. I try to think success, not failure—to "see" good shots, not bad ones. And I do try very hard to keep my mind on golf, on what I'm supposed to be doing at that moment, not on what happened yesterday or on the last hole, or what might happen tomorrow or on the next hole.

Other types of personalities have different ways of combatting tensions. I'm sure Arnold Palmer has often relieved his by mentally deciding that he was going to literally *force* the course into submission and hang the consequences. It's a do-or-die approach that I've often seen written all over his face. Lee Trevino, on the other hand, relieves his tensions by talking all the time, to other people, to himself, even sometimes in midswing. Man, how he talks! I think Gary Player's physical fitness routines are tension-relievers. They make him feel prepared, confident. When the screws tighten on Gary, I wouldn't be surprised if he switches his mind onto things like two-mile runs or hundreds of pushups with a suitcase on his back.

Every different personality, I guess, can use a different kind of mental gimmick to promote staying loose over the ball. But whatever peg you might choose, its effectiveness will be directly related to how well it builds your concentration and confidence and, in the final analysis, how well you can discipline yourself.

CHAPTER 3

The Full-Shot Swing: Starting Back

The old maxim that the entire swing is governed by its first few inches is certainly true in my case. I can sometimes instinctively make midswing compensations to produce an effective shot after a poor start but, generally, when I start back incorrectly I hit a mediocre shot.

In fact, the longest slump in my career was caused by an incorrect takeaway movement that became habitual and thus very difficult to cure. It began in 1967, lasted through the better part of 1970, and ultimately was responsible for the way I now "trigger" the swing.

At the top of the backswing I want the club to parallel the line along which it will swing at impact. To explain this better, let's assume that I tried to hit every shot straight, and that I always swung the clubshaft to a horizontal position at the top of the backswing. In that case, at the top of every swing I'd always want the shaft to parallel the target line. The reason is that the club would thus have maintained a reciprocating straight-line motion to its arc during the backswing. Unless I made a movement in my forward swing that upset the relationship, it would do the same thing coming down.

Let's put this another way in the hope that we can make it clear. I want the *arc* the clubhead describes to maintain a constant relationship to my *target line* back and through. The alignment of the shaft at the top of the swing, relative to my target line, is an indicator of whether or not this is happening. If the shaft parallels my target line at the top, all's well. But if the shaft points left or

101

GOLF MY WAY
Jack Nicklaus

A number of great golfers have "crossed the line" at the top of the backswing, then looped or dropped the club back on track during the downswing. I can't handle such maneuvers. For me to play my best, the arc described by the clubhead must maintain a constant relationship to my target line from takeaway to impact. I achieve that constant relationship by setting the club shaft parallel to my target line at the top of the backswing. If the club points right or left of target at the top I'm in trouble, because the forward-swing path reciprocates my backswing path and delivers the clubhead across, not along, my target line during impact.

right of my target line at the top I'm in trouble, because a forward-swing arc reciprocating the backswing arc will deliver the clubhead *across,* not along, my target line at impact. If the club points right of my target at the top, the forward swing arc will deliver the clubhead to the ball from inside to outside my target line. The reverse is also true: If, at the top, I have pointed the club left of my target line, the reciprocating forward-swing arc will deliver the clubhead to the ball from outside to inside the target line.

WILY WAY TO WAGGLE

I'm not a great waggler of the club, but some tour players and many teachers swear by it as a means of breaking down tension and of "programming" the swing. When I have waggled, I've found a slight shifting of the weight from foot to foot, in tune with the to-and-froing of the club, to be very helpful in keeping my leg muscles fluid.

If you do waggle, let the action help you preview the shot you're going to play by waggling along the desired swing path; thus, out-to-in waggles for a fade and in-to-out waggles for a draw.

I'm afraid this is not easy to explain, but I hope you get the point, which is really that, if my club at the top of the swing doesn't parallel my target line, I won't hit the ball correctly unless I somehow correct the club's arc on the forward swing.

Some golfers adjust very effectively for such "crossing of the line." Bob Jones pointed the club well to the right of target at the top, and compensated by looping the club toward the outside as he swung down. I believe that at one time Ben Hogan set the club the other way at the top—left of his target line—and compensated by "dropping" it very much inside as he initiated the forward swing. Personally, however, I am scared stiff of compensations; for me golf is difficult enough already. Thus it has always been my principle to try to set the club parallel to my target line at the top, from where it will most *naturally* swing squarely into the back of the ball.

Sometime in 1967, for no immediately apparent reason, I began to have great difficulty in doing that. Try as I might to swing the club back so that in descent it moved along the target line up to impact, I ended up swinging it across the line from inside to outside—toward right of target. I was still basically committed to a fading technique at that time, but you try fading when the club moves into the ball from *inside* your intended line. No way! As the days and weeks passed and I could never seem to correct the problem permanently, I became increasingly frustrated as a person and increasingly inconsistent as a player.

To cut a long story short, I eventually discovered that the fault sprang from a change of shoulder alignment at the very start of the backswing. This alteration originated in the way I actually began the swing.

Every golfer needs something to "trigger" his swing. It is almost impossible to begin the swing slowly and smoothly from cold—from a dead halt at address. Good golfers use all sorts of "triggering" techniques. Gary Player "kicks in" his right knee. Julius Boros does almost a soft-shoe shuffle as he gets ready to take off. The most common "trigger" on tour is the forward press: a slight inclination of the hands or the left side toward the target, from which the golfer, in effect, "rebounds" into his backswing.

Instead of this kind of forward press, throughout my career I had used what I call a "stationary press." This was simply an increase of hand pressure on the shaft, a firming up of the grip just before I started the club away from the ball.

That was my chief swing "trigger," but I combined with it a movement common to many tour professionals, and particularly pronounced in Sam Snead. Just before we start back, Sam and I very noticeably swivel our chins to the right. Correctly executed, this movement isn't in any sense a head lift or sway, but simply a swiveling motion. The axis of the neck stays put, but the chin turns a few inches to the right. In Sam's case and mine, and I imagine in most other golfers who use the movement, its purpose is, first, to allow the fullest possible turn of the shoulders on the backswing, and second, to brace the head against swaying toward the target on the forward swing.

Club players know only too well how easy it is in golf to overdo a good thing—to destroy the value of a once-helpful action simply by exaggerating it. That is precisely what I had fallen into the habit of doing with my stationary press and my swiveling head.

If you take a club, grip it lightly, put yourself into the address position, then firm up your hands on the club a few times, you may find that the squeezing action tends to pull your left shoulder forward and your right shoulder back; to, in effect, "close" your shoulders—align them more to the right of your target. Now, still at address, swivel your chin to the right a few times. If you swivel it on a path parallel to your target line, your shoulders will move on the same path. But if your swivel is toward the *inside* of your target line, again your shoulders will be pulled into a *closed* alignment relative to the target line.

I had a devil of a time discovering these faults. I would align my shoulders a little open or square at address and *know* I had done so—no possible mistake there. But by the time I had finished stationary pressing and swiveling my chin in getting the swing under way, my shoulders had, in fact, been pulled into a

DRAGGING AND COCKING

Dragging the hands back before the clubhead moved didn't stop a few olden-day golfers from playing well, but you don't see this "lagging" type of takeaway on tour very much today. Its danger is that it produces a varying takeaway path and thus an inconsistent swing plane and arc that can lead to all kinds of mistakes.

More common is the opposite maneuver, an early wrist break—or even, in former PGA champion Jerry Barber's case, a wrist break that actually starts the backswing. To me, this is a contrived and unnatural motion that destroys over-all coordination, leading to inconsistency. Thus I avoid it.

closed position: aimed *right* of target. Result: a crossing of the line at the top of the backswing, many poor shots, and much frustration.

The results of this discovery were twofold. First, I now regularly check to see that, in swiveling my chin at the start of the backswing, I turn it on a line parallel with my target line, not inside that line. Second, I scrapped the stationary press and adopted a forward press as my swing "trigger"—a movement designed not merely to set me in motion smoothly, but to safeguard against working into a closed-shoulder alignment during the takeaway. I achieve this by gently "pressing" my entire body and the club, not only toward the target—as do most forward pressers—but forward *and slightly left* of the target. The angle is very slightly left, but enough to insure that my shoulders don't realign themselves "inside" as I rebound into the takeaway.

Such can be the importance of proper alignment at the start of the swing.

I believe you cannot start the golf club back too slowly, provided you *swing* it back rather than *take* it away from the ball. I said in a previous book that the ideal swing start is a "terribly forced, ridiculously slow movement of the club away from the ball." I still feel that way. The harder I want to swing, the slower I try to start back. But on *every* shot I endeavor to swing the club into motion very deliberately, very positively, only just fast enough to avoid jerkiness. Obviously the motion speeds up as my backswing develops, but the slower I can keep it those first few feet of the takeaway the better I'll play.

Reasons? Primarily three. First, the slower you start back, the better your chance of moving the clubhead on a particular line, and thus the better your chance of establishing the particular arc and plane you desire. Second, the slower you start back, the easier it is to coordinate or unify the movements of the feet, legs, hips, hands, arms, and shoulders; the better your chance of starting back in "one piece." Third, the slower you start back—while still *swinging the club,* mind you—the smoother the over-all tempo you'll establish. Let's take a closer look at these factors.

Many golfers get confused about the line along which the club should start back, particularly when they have been made conscious of "hitting from the inside." (In pro-ams you see a lot of golfers almost wiping out their right ankle, they whip the club back so sharply "inside." The inevitable result is that, in trying to get back on line coming down, they throw the club "outside.")

If you've stayed with me thus far in this book, you must know that I start the club back neither "inside" nor "outside," but *straight along a backward extension of the line on which I want the ball to take off.* Another way to put this would be to say I start the club straight back along a line parallel to my shoulders.

If I am intending to fade the ball, my shoulders will be aligned left of target. My start-back line will then, of course, actually be a little *outside the direct ball-to-target line.* Conversely, if I am endeavoring to draw the ball, my shoulders will be aligned a little right of target. My start-back line will then be a little *inside the direct ball-to-target line.* The point is that in each case my start-back line *matches my shoulder alignment* at address—*not* the ball-to-target line. Only if I were trying to hit the ball straight would the start-back line and the direct ball-to-target line coincide.

I may be laboring this point, but it has to be stressed if we are going to eradicate the many confusions that exist about the club's correct start-back path. What the golfer has to clearly understand is that "straight back" and "straight through" must relate to *his direction of aim,* not to his direct ball-target line, unless he's trying to hit the shot dead straight.

Now let's see if we can clear up another frequently pretzeled point: where the club should go once it has traveled a foot or two straight back. To do so, let's make a little experiment. Take a club, assume your address position, then place the toe of the club against a wall. You're going to try to hit this shot dead straight; thus the wall represents both the ball-target line and your start-back path. Now swing the club back slowly in such a way that you keep it on that line throughout—in other words, keep its toe touching the wall all the time. Feel like a golf swing? No way, right? Okay, now make a full swing touching

Assuming the golfer swings the club back from the ball with a sound "one-piece" movement from a sound setup position, the clubhead will move "inside" the target line without any attempt to manipulate it in that direction. How much and how quickly it does so will be determined chiefly by the distance the golfer stands from the ball. For example, Tom Weiskopf, at 6 feet 3 inches, must stand closer to the ball than 5-foot-8-inch Gary Player. Thus Weiskopf's natural swing is more upright than Player's, and Tom's club moves inside the target line later than Gary's.

the toe of the club to the wall only for the first 6 inches to a foot, then let the clubhead go wherever it wants. The farther you swing back, the farther the club moves "inside." Right? *Right!* And that's just how it should happen on the course.

The fact is, how soon and how much a golfer swings "inside" depends solely on the distance he stands from the ball, and on the degree of his shoulder and hip turn. Obviously, every golfer moves inside earliest and farthest with the driver, because he stands farthest from the ball when using the longest club in the bag. Equally obviously, a flat swinger will move inside earlier and farther with *every* club than an upright swinger. But, in all instances, the amount of "insideness"—the plane of the swing—is correctly determined by the golfer's distance from the ball and his body turn, not by some contrived or conscious manipulation of the club in a particular direction. Or, at least, that's the way it should be.

"Taking the club back in one piece" is golfing jargon for keeping each part of the body in step with all the others at the beginning of the swing. I am a "one piece" man, because I believe that moving everything back together does four important things:

1. It sets the club moving on the correct "straight back" path that will be reciprocated by a "straight through" path at impact.
2. Its sets up the wide, full, swing arc essential to generate leverage.
3. It prevents a lazy, "hands-and-arms only" kind of swing by forcing the hips and shoulders to turn.
4. It establishes good over-all swing tempo by encouraging a smooth, slow, deliberate start-up pace.

To give you an idea of what "one piece" means to me, I'll try to describe what I feel happens on a full shot from the moment I rebound from my slight forward press until my hands reach about hip height on the backswing.

The clubhead starts back first, but only infinitesimally before my hands and arms begin to move the shaft. My left arm and the club retain the straight-line relationship they formed at address, with no wrist hinging becoming visible until my hands reach about hip height, when the weight of the club will naturally begin to hinge or cock the wrists.

I feel that my left arm and the club are moving almost entirely as a result of being *pushed* back by my left shoulder as it begins to turn *down* under my chin. My left arm's swinging motion never "gets ahead of" the left shoulder's pushing motion at this point. I am unaware of my right arm; its role is entirely passive. It simply follows the lead of, and ultimately acts as a brace for, the left arm.

The clubhead travels straight back on a path parallel to my shoulders until their turning causes it to start swinging "inside" naturally. How far the clubhead moves back directly on line before going inside depends on the length of club I'm using; the wedge obviously stays on the target line longer than the driver because I'm nearer to the ball at address.

While the clubhead is traveling on the target line, its face remains square to that path. As the clubhead swings progressively more "inside," however, the club's face appears to "open" gradually—it looks increasingly to the right of the target. This is not a result of any manipulation of the club by my hands, wrists, and arms. They have not rolled or maneuvered the club in any way; they bear exactly the same angular relationship to the clubface as they did at address. The apparent "opening" of the club is simply a natural result of my body turning.

As my hands pass my flexed right knee, the combined forces of my turning left shoulder and extending left arm begin to pull my left knee toward my right knee. This, in turn, causes my left foot to start rolling onto its inside edge. My right knee remains flexed and does not move laterally, and thus serves as a brace against my upper body's turning. However, the knee does move a little to the rear as the body turn proceeds, just sufficiently to prevent rigidity (which is to be avoided at any point in the swing in any part of the body). While I felt an increase of weight on the inside of the right foot very soon after the club started back, now that weight is increasing sharply. Also at about this point my hips are beginning to turn, to allow my shoulders to continue turning. But all these lower-body actions are *permitted,* not *encouraged.* They happen only in response to the forces acting above.

By the time my hands have reached hip height, my shoulders have turned about 70 degrees, my hips about 30 degrees, and my left knee is approximately opposite the ball. My left shoulder is almost under my "cocked" chin, and my head, of course, is very still. My left arm is extended as far as it will go from my body and, ideally, the club and my left arm still form a straight line—no wrist hinging yet. My right arm, still passive, has moved well away from my side to allow full extension of the left arm, but my right elbow does not "fly." It points down, not behind me.

I have not consciously manipulated the club in any way, but the turning of my hips and shoulders will have caused a slight clockwise rotation of my left wrist and forearm, so that the back of my left hand now faces outward, paralleling the target line. Thus the clubface also "looks" outward—is between a one- and two-o'clock position as one looks down at it. But the back of my left hand and left forearm still form a straight line, as they did at address: no hinging, no convex or concave kinks at the wrist. Thus any "opening" of the clubface that has occurred is simply a natural response to the action of my body.

To break down a section of the swing like this for descriptive purposes could give the impression that I swing like a clockwork man: *"Click*—A position achieved; *click*—B position achieved; *click*—C position achieved; okay for D." The truth is the exact opposite. Although what I've described takes place relatively slowly—in about half a second—it is a very compact and flowing *one-piece* action.

You should keep that in mind any time you work on your own takeaway. Even though on the practice tee you might be able to dismantle this phase of the swing for servicing, by the time you get on the course it had better be all back together again in one piece.

The Full-Shot Swing:
To the Top

Once the club has moved back to hip height the mood of the shot is set, usually irrevocably. You can rarely consciously direct your movements any longer. You are committed to a chain reaction of events, each determined by its predecessor. The setup governs the takeaway; the takeaway governs the backswing; the backswing will govern the forward swing, and the forward swing governs the destiny of the ball.

Thus, what happens after the point where I left myself at the end of the previous chapter—about a third of the way back from the ball on a full shot—is directed by my instincts, not my will. Perhaps if I sense something is out of whack in my setup or takeaway—and, remember, I can see the club start back with my peripheral vision—I'll try to compensate later in the backswing. But generally, if I have set up correctly and made a good start, my concentration will be focused on maintaining smooth tempo and hitting the ball hard and solidly.

However, let us take an analytical look at what I feel does actually happen during the next segment of my swing, from about halfway back on the backswing to the beginning of the forward swing. But first let me refresh your memory about my over-all backswing objectives. They are:

1. An upright plane to give myself the best chance of delivering the club to the ball while traveling along my target line.

2. The minimum disruption of that plane as it was established by my setup and takeaway, again to give myself the best chance of delivering the clubhead correctly at impact.

. The widest possible arc consistent with keeping the top of my spine "centered," to help me generate maximum leverage and thus maximum club-head speed.

. The fullest possible body turn consistent with a fixed swing axis, again to develop maximum leverage and, as a result, clubhead speed.

Okay, now back into action. We'll probably paint the clearest picture by looking at the various components separately, but please keep in mind that what I'm describing all happens in a fraction of a second and that each action synchronizes with and flows into all the others.

FEET.   The farther my shoulders turn and the higher my arms swing, the more weight moves onto the inside of my right foot, and the more the weight remaining on my left foot rolls (through a hinging of the ankle) onto its inside edge. At the ultimate stretching or coiling point in the backswing with the driver, three-wood, and sometimes a long iron, my left heel rises a little way off the ground. On less than full shots, the entire *inside* edge of the left heel remains on the ground. I would prefer it to remain fixed on shots with the long clubs,

IF YOU WANT TO SWING UPRIGHT, DON'T "TUCK IN" YOUR RIGHT ELBOW

If you seek an upright swing plane, beware of that old tenet about tucking your right elbow into your side on the backswing.

To maintain an upright plane, the left arm must swing *away* from the body, the left shoulder must move *down* (not merely around), and the right shoulder must move *up* and around.

If the right arm hugs the body, the left arm will follow it, and so will the shoulders—the left shoulder will move around rather than down. Result: Your clubhead will move quickly "inside" your target line, and you will swing "flat," even though you may have set up to swing "upright."

DOWN THE FAIRWAY

NEAT WAY TO TRAIN THE RIGHT KNEE

Keeping the right knee slightly flexed yet firmly in position during the backswing is tough for many golfers. The trick is to set and keep your weight on the *inside* of the right foot. If your weight moves over to the outside of the foot, the knee is bound either to stiffen or buckle outward.

To help you to learn the correct "feel," stick a golf ball under the outside part of your right instep on the practice tee. It will cant the foot and the knee inward, and you'll learn what it really feels like to "coil the spring" on the backswing.

too, if I could still make a big enough turn. At the top of the swing, I feel that a high proportion of my weight is on the inside edge of my right foot and that the remainder is on the inside edge of my left foot.

LEGS.   My right leg increases its anchoring and stabilizing role in direct proportion to the increasing stretching and coiling forces being applied up above. The knee remains flexed and resilient, moving slightly to the rear but never laterally. Again in direct proportion to the forces exerted on it by my upper-body actions, the left knee bends and shifts over toward the right knee. At the top of the swing with a driver, my left knee points to a spot a good foot or more behind the ball.

HIPS.   My hips turn as far away from the target as they will go without forcing my right leg to straighten or collapse, or throwing my weight to the outside of my right foot. At the completion of the backswing, my hips have turned at least 45 degrees—possibly more. Certainly on a full drive my left hip has turned well behind the ball.

Because my shoulders turn on a very upright plane—nearer to vertical than horizontal—my hips also turn on a slightly tilted plane. The left hip is thus a little lower than the right at the completion of the backswing.

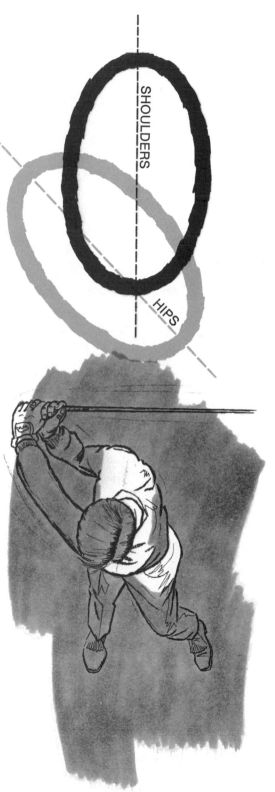

So long as a golfer doesn't sway his head, straighten his right knee, or shift his weight onto the outside of his right foot, the farther he can turn his hips and shoulders going back, the more leverage he will generate, and thus the farther he will hit the ball. I turn my shoulders through about 110 degrees and my hips through up to 60 degrees on full drives. A 90-degree shoulder turn combined with about half that amount of hip turn (shown here) represents the norm among today's top tour players.

SHOULDERS

HIPS

WHY MINIMUM LEFT-HEEL LIFT?

Do not make the mistake of deliberately raising your left heel. Simply allow it to be pulled off the ground by your turn and swing on full shots, for two reasons.

If you deliberately raise the left heel high, you run the risk of involuntarily raising everything else higher than it was at address, and this obviously will distort your swing arc.

Also, the higher the left heel lifts on the backswing, the more difficult it is to replace the left foot back where it was at address at the start of the forward swing. And since the left foot must resist some very powerful forward-swing thrusting by the legs and hips, it should return to the stable, workmanlike position where you first put it.

SHOULDERS.   Even when my hips have stopped turning, my shoulders continue to turn and coil. In fact, I want to turn my shoulders as far as they will possibly go short of forcing my right knee to collapse or stiffen, or my weight to move from the inside to the outside of the right foot, or my left heel to rise more than about an inch from the ground.

What it all adds up to is a very big shoulder turn. At the top of the driver swing, particularly when I'm intent largely on distance, I'd say my shoulders often have turned through at least 110 degrees.

ARMS.   In the early part of the backswing, my shoulders are "pushing" my arms along, even though I am simultaneously stretching my left arm away from my body. At a point roughly two thirds of the way through the backswing, this shoulder-arm relationship has switched. Now, because the weight of the club is swinging my arms and because I'm still stretching the left arm, my arms are "pulling" my shoulders around to squeeze the last few inches of turn out of them. I want my hands to go as high as possible. I like to have the feeling, as I near the top of the backswing, of trying to thrust them through the clouds. I just cannot get them too high. In actual fact, my hands usually reach a point directly behind and about 6 inches above my head with the driver.

WRISTS.   Nothing happens to my wrists on a full shot until they reach about hip height. Until then they retain the same angular relationship to my hands and arms that they had at address. But, as the club starts to swing upward as well as backward as it passes hip height, the momentum of the moving club-head begins to cause a gradual hinging or cocking of the wrists.

I make no effort either to encourage or prevent this hinging action at any point in the backswing—I just let it happen. However, because of my comparatively firm grip on the club, the rate of this wrist hinging is relatively slow. In fact, it doesn't become complete until my hands have reached their highest point in the backswing, when the weight of the clubhead is exerting its strongest wrist-cocking force.

GOOD AND BAD WAYS TO EXTEND THE ARC

There are three ways to extend the backswing arc. Club golfers often choose the two worst.

The worst way of all to lengthen your backswing is to loosen your hands at the top, causing the club to dip or drop or otherwise flop around. Your shots may go a long way, but unless you're lucky enough to regrip the club exactly as you held it at address, they'll go just about anywhere except on target.

Almost as bad a way of getting the club back is bending the left arm. It's a lazy way to swing that not only reduces power, but also causes much the same sort of erratic shots as does loosening the grip at the top.

The best way to extend your backswing arc is to keep your hands firm and your left arm straight (but not stiff), then simply increase your hip and shoulder turn. Take it from me that a swing in which the shoulders turn through 90 degrees or more, even though the club falls short of horizontal at the top, will be a lot more powerful than a swing in which the club drops way below horizontal but the left shoulder fails to turn past the ball on your backswing.

NO "PAUSE" AT THE TOP

Should you "pause" at the top of the backswing?

Some good players have appeared to do so—Cary Middle-coff seemed even to come to a complete stop—but I don't buy the idea. The way I play golf, there really is no top of the back-swing. When I swing, my feet, legs, and hips begin to initiate the forward swing before my hands reach their highest level or my shoulders finish turning.

At the top I do have a momentary feeling of "waiting" with my hands, arms and shoulders: waiting for the lower body to start its work. But if I actually "paused" at the top—literally stopped everything, even for a split second—the best I could do would be to make a weak pass at the ball with my hands and arms. That's not the way to win long-driving contests.

HANDS.   By the time my hands have reached hip height, the back of the left hand is facing forward—away from me—but it is still in line with my left fore-arm; there has been no concave kinking or convex arching at the back of the wrist. As the swinging weight of the clubhead gradually cocks the wrists, ideally the back of my left hand and forearm still remain in a straight line—still no concavity or convexity at the back of the wrist. Ideally, this same straight-line back-of-left-hand/left-forearm relationship is preserved right through to the completion of the backswing. Thus, when I'm "right" at the top, the back of my hands, my wrists, and my arms still bear the same angular relationship to the clubface as they did at address; and, if I don't manipulate them coming down, they should maintain the same relationship through impact.

HEAD.   My neck—the axis of the swing—has remained where it was at address, even though my chin did swivel to the right at the start of the take-away. I can almost feel my left shoulder touching my chin, and I am looking at the ball through my left eye because my nose blocks my right eye's view of it.

Those, then, are my backswing moves, positions, and feelings. Remember that all of this—from forward press to full windup—occurs in about one second, hopefully *smoothly and compactly*.

How do I "feel" over-all at the top of the backswing? I feel strong, exerted, stretched, coiled, wound up, packed full of leverage—not tense, but springy, like a sprinter set for a 100-yard dash. In short, I feel good and ready to send that little white ball on a nice long journey.

And now, if I may, a few comments related to that most frequently analyzed of all golfing positions, the angle or alignment of the clubface at the top of the backswing.

Some of the action photographs of myself used by golf magazines in recent years, to make technical or instructional points, really make me want to laugh—or cry. I have no objection to people publishing pictures of me playing golf, and I'm not too concerned with what they say about my game. But, for the sake of their readers, I do wish they'd relate the pictures to the kind of shots I'm hitting and the general state of my game when they were taken. I'm sure other tour players feel the same way about this.

I remember the well-known and very competent West Coast golf photographer, Chuck Brenkus, taking dozens of shots of me at Las Vegas three or four years ago. In all honesty, I've hardly ever swung as poorly as I did then. I couldn't make even a half-decent hip turn on the backswing. I couldn't "get

HOW TO AVOID "FIRE AND FALL BACK"

One of golf's nastier sights is the "out and over" downswing of the long handicapper. It often results from a *hip sway* instead of a *hip turn* on the backswing.

When a golfer sways his hips laterally away from the target going back, the chances are fifty to one that he'll immediately spin around his right hip and heel as he starts his forward swing. Unable to get his weight off his right foot, he's committed to an ugly "fire and fall back" routine, featuring a pronounced "out and over" movement of the right shoulder and a resulting outside-in clubhead path through impact.

The cure is simple and usually very effective. On your backswing think of the lower spine as an axis, and *turn* your hips around that axis without letting any weight shift onto the outside of your right foot.

THE HIPS MUST TURN

I understand there's a theory in golf today that the hips shouldn't turn on the backswing. The idea seems to be that the less you turn your hips, while still turning your shoulders, the more leverage you'll generate.

It's hogwash, and here's why. Stand erect with your arms at your sides and keep them there. Now hold your hips still and turn your shoulders. Impossible, right? Even the slightest shoulder turn forces *some* hip turn. And the more the shoulders turn, the more the hips are forced to turn, right? Of course—because that's the way *homo sapiens* is made, unless he's incredibly supple or some kind of contortionist.

Thus you should never try to restrict your hip turn if you want to hit the ball a long way. Simply keep your right knee flexed, your weight on the inside of your right foot, and your left heel as low as possible; then turn those hips as far as they'll go in harness with your turning shoulders.

What actually happens in most good swings is that the shoulders ultimately *out turn* the hips (perhaps that's what our "still hips" friends really mean). But there must be a generous hip turn, too, if the golfer is going to move into the ball correctly on the forward swing. In fact, if I didn't turn my hips going back, I'd never be able to use my legs correctly coming down. I'd be forced to throw the club "out and over" with my shoulders on every shot.

One point to watch, however: Don't let the *speed* of your hip turn on the backswing exceed the speed of your shoulder turn. Turn both simultaneously. If your hips turn faster than your shoulders, you'll tend to swing flat and bring your wrists into the act too quickly.

HOW FAR BACK?

How far should you swing back? As far as you can without collapsing, stiffening or swaying your right knee (although it can move rearward), lifting your left heel way up, bending your left arm, or loosening your grip at the top.

If you meet these requirements, I don't care if the club touches your left ankle on the backswing; you're still not over-swinging. What you are doing is using a very supple body to make a big shoulder and hip turn, as many fine women golfers do.

I've heard it said that I "overswing." I really don't, but I'm glad some people think I do because it indicates I have a very *full* swing. And if you want to know how important that is, take a run through golf's history books. You will come across few great champions with short swings, especially among those who have lasted long enough to win seniors' tournaments. I feel that golfers with relatively long backswings, if properly executed, tend better to resist the adverse effects of swing shortening that seem to occur in later life.

out of my own way" going back, as the saying goes. The result was that my left wrist was bent back, or arched, repeatedly putting my clubface into a "closed" position at the top of the swing. I really was hitting the ball all over creation at that time. And—lo and behold!—one day I pick up a golf magazine, and there are those same pictures of me, captioned something like "Jack Nicklaus in perfect top-of-the-backswing position." What a gas! Chuck just took good pictures of a bad swing.

The fact is, there is one top-of-the-swing clubface position from which I can play well, one from which I can play decently, and one from which I'm almost certain to be rooting around in the rhubarb a great deal.

My ideal top-of-the-swing clubface position is straight, or "square": The clubface is aligned roughly midway between horizontal and vertical. I most often attain it when the back of my left hand and my left forearm are in a straight line—no bend in the wrist—at the top. From here, I can fade or draw

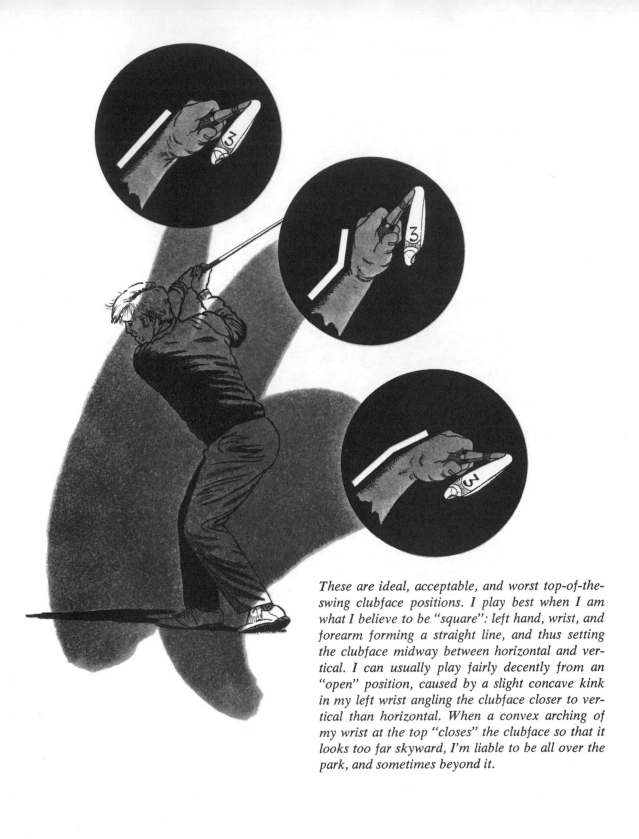

These are ideal, acceptable, and worst top-of-the-swing clubface positions. I play best when I am what I believe to be "square": left hand, wrist, and forearm forming a straight line, and thus setting the clubface midway between horizontal and vertical. I can usually play fairly decently from an "open" position, caused by a slight concave kink in my left wrist angling the clubface closer to vertical than horizontal. When a convex arching of my wrist at the top "closes" the clubface so that it looks too far skyward, I'm liable to be all over the park, and sometimes beyond it.

the ball at will, depending on my setup and which actions I emphasize coming down.

My less ideal but acceptable top-of-the-swing clubface position is "open": The clubface is aligned nearer to vertical than to horizontal—its face looking more forward than upward. I attain this position most often when there is a slight concave kink in my left wrist at the top. It is a very "safe" position for a fade, but I can also draw from here simply by releasing the clubhead a little earlier in the forward swing.

My *worst* top-of-the-swing clubface position is "closed": The clubface is aligned nearer to horizontal than to vertical—its face looking more upward than forward. I attain this position when there is a convex bend, or outward "arch," in my left wrist at the top of the swing. From that position, I can hit the ball left to right, right to left, straight left, straight right, left to left, right to right—anywhere in the world on any given swing.

The truth is that except on certain "type" shots, I avoid the arched-wrist, closed-clubface position at the top like the plague. A few golfers have used it very successfully: Arnold Palmer did and Lee Trevino still does. But, as I have said earlier in this book, the closed-to-open way of playing golf is not for me. It demands too much strength; too much manipulation of the club both going back and coming forward; too fine a degree of timing. I believe that's why Arnold has changed as he's gotten older, and why Lee will probably change as he, too, gets older. And I believe it's why you see all the finest senior amateur golfers playing with a "square-to-open" clubface at the top. If they didn't, they'd have given up competitive golf years ago.

CHAPTER 5

The Full-Shot Swing: To Impact

I have never tried to swing back and then "hold" my top-of-the-backswing position for any length of time. I doubt very much if I could do so for more than maybe a second or two. I'm so stretched and coiled at the top that I'm literally *forced* to react and start down. In fact, thinking about it, I'd hesitate about trying to hold my full-shot, top-of-the-swing position beyond a second or two even for experimental purposes. So many muscles are under such heavy stress at this point that I'd be scared of tearing or straining something.

I make this point to indicate just how *reflexive* the forward swing actions are if the backswing has been correctly executed. It's just like that tree analogy we used way back to try to explain my concept of leverage. You cut the rope, and *Whoooosh!*—the ball's on its way.

In this light, obviously, the movements that comprise the forward swing cannot be made with much conscious direction. The downswing is much more instinctive, much more a matter of "feel," than the backswing. The interplay of the muscles is too complex, and it happens too quickly, for the downswing to be consciously directed. Even a relatively slow swinger takes only about half a second to return the club from the top of his swing to the ball. Obviously, therefore, no golfer can actually "think" his way back to impact once he's started down, even though some—including top professionals—may believe they do!

As many readers will know only too well, the transition from backswing to forward swing is the most critical, and difficult, phase of the golf swing. The slightest false move here can destroy all the good work that's gone before.

That's why I'm sure that even the best players, while planning shots at address, use such a wide and ever-changing variety of "start down" gimmicks. For example, I bet if you asked each player on tour what thoughts or "feels" he uses to begin the forward swing, you'd get twice as long a list than if you asked for mental pictures or gimmicks relating to any other part of the swing. I know that in my own case I'll employ any one of about half a dozen start-down "feels" as I plan the swing.

I have a pretty good idea of what actually occurs during my forward swing and, as with the takeaway and backswing, I think the easiest way to paint a comprehensive picture is to break the over-all movement down into segments. Again, though, let me stress—especially for you eager analysts of stop-action, swing-sequence pictures—that we are talking about *reflexive action*. It is impossible for a golfer to consciously "put" himself into the positions I describe. He can swing through them only by *reacting* to previously correct actions.

As I said in the previous chapter, my forward swing actually commences in my lower body before my upper body has completed the backswing. It's a sort of "two-way stretch" effect in which, as my shoulders reach the extremity

FORCING THE LEGS TO WORK

Sometimes, when I've laid off golf for a while, my legs aren't in any condition to work correctly in my forward swing. Then I'm in the same boat as the fellow who rides a car or sits in an office all week and wonders why his shoulders "come over" the ball on Saturday mornings.

Here's what I do. Until I get my legs back in shape through practicing and playing, or exercising, I try to keep the upward movement of my left shoulder as slow as possible on my forward swing. What this does is give my legs a little more time to move laterally toward the target before my shoulders have a chance to take over the swing involuntarily and ruin the shot.

If you can keep that upward left-shoulder movement relatively slow as you start back to the ball, you'll find that your legs are virtually forced to work toward the target.

of their turn and my hands their highest point somewhere up behind my head, my feet, legs and hips have already begun to thrust toward the target. But here's how I "feel" my downswing piece by piece, so to speak:

STARTING DOWN.   As the very first movement of the forward swing, my left heel, if it has come clear of the ground at all, socks back to earth. Simultaneously, I begin to move my weight *laterally* from right to left across to the *inside* of my left foot by pushing hard off the inside of my right foot. This initial shifting of weight to the left side pulls my left knee *laterally* back toward the target—photos prove that it actually moves back to a position well forward of the ball before my hands have descended even a few inches.

This powerful—but hopefully smooth—burst of foot and leg action toward the target has two effects. First, because it starts just before my arms reverse direction, it creates a further "coiling of the spring." Second, since the clubhead's weight is still moving away from the ball, this reversal of direction also hinges or cocks my wrists a little more.

Very quickly, the forward thrust in my feet and legs forces my shoulders to change their backswing directions. My left shoulder, which had been going

THINKING "LEFT" AND "RIGHT"

I'm a "left-sided" golfer, but I never hesitate to think in right-sided terms if my left-sided thoughts aren't working.

For example, if I can't get the correct hip turn going back by thinking "turn the left hip," I'll think "pull the right hip out of the way." The same sort of thing often applies with the shoulders on the forward swing. My preferred thought is "move the left shoulder up and the left hip around." But if that doesn't seem to be working, I'll try "move the right shoulder down and the right hip around."

So long as the desired effect is achieved, I don't think it matters at all which "side" you think about. In fact, it's probably good to switch patterns occasionally, for the sake of striking a balance. Thinking one side or the other all the time can easily lead to exaggeration of a particular move.

back and down, begins to be pulled forward and up. The right shoulder, which had been turning up and forward, begins to be pulled down and away from the target.

Let me emphasize here yet again that these initiating movements are

After the takeaway, the transition from backswing to downswing is the most critical move in golf. If a golfer does not initiate his downward/forward motion with a toward-the-target shuttling or thrusting of the legs, it becomes almost impossible for him (a) to swing the clubhead along, rather than across, the target line; and (b) to retain its maximum speed until impact.

totally reflexive. They happen spontaneously—a virtually irresistible "release" of the powerful backswing coiling and winding forces.

SEQUENCE OF MOTION.   Correctly executed, the forward-swing initiating movements establish a highly desirable sequence, or chain reaction, of events that continues right on through to impact and beyond. To capture the essence of this sequence, let's relate it to the old spiritual that told us, "The foot bone's connected to the heel bone, the heel bone's connected to the ankle bone, the ankle bone's connected to the shin bone, the shin bone's connected to the knee bone, the knee bone's connected to the thigh bone . . ." and so on, right up to the head bone.

In my forward swing, just as in the song, the feet lead, by initiating my toward-the-target weight shift. Then my ankles follow my feet by rolling toward the target. Then my knees follow my ankles, shuttling laterally toward the target. Then my thighs, and through them my hips, follow my knees—again shuttling or sliding *laterally* toward the target. Trailing along behind the hips come my shoulders, the left being pulled up and the right down by the increasingly powerful *lateral* thrusting of my legs and hips. Behind the shoulders come my arms, swinging down and forward but still trailing the shoulders. Then trailing my arms comes the shaft of the club—still an extension of my left arm, mind you, still the outer end of a long lever from my left shoulder to the clubhead, even though it's now hinged in the middle by my wrists. Finally, last of all, along comes the clubhead, just as in the song: "The neck bone's connected to the head bone, now hear the word of the Lord."

FULL THROTTLE.   Once the swing has totally changed direction and I put on full throttle, it is *always* my legs and hips that motivate the club. Think how pressing the gas pedal on your car causes the engine to drive the transmission shaft faster and faster. Similarly, my thrusting legs and hips, by forcing my shoulders to turn, drive my arms and the club faster and faster. Finally, just before impact, I reach a point where no further acceleration is possible and, because of centrifugal force, I *must* release the club into the ball. At that point my wrists are forced to unhinge spontaneously.

That's the over-all picture, the start and the sequence of the forward swing. Now let's backtrack a bit and try to describe what I think actually takes place anatomically as the accelerator hits the floor.

My legs continue to thrust or shuttle *laterally* toward the target until my hands have been pulled down to about waist height. Normally, I have a distinct feeling that my left shoulder is moving up and my right shoulder is moving down as a consequence of my *lateral* leg thrust. Occasionally, depend-

"TOLLING THE BELL"

A common start-down thought on tour is to pull downward with the left arm—"tolling the bell." It's fine, so long as the left arm doesn't bend as it pulls, and so long as the legs work in harness with the pulling action.

If the left arm bends, you'll destroy your leverage as well as your swing arc. If your legs don't move ahead of your upper body, your right shoulder will be forced forward and you'll swing "over" the ball.

ing on how I'm playing, I'll reverse this emphasis: I'll think of my right shoulder moving down and my left going up. Either way, my shoulders must return on the same relatively steep plane of their backswing turn; I never want the feeling that they are traveling "around" instead of up and down.

Normally, I have the feeling that my right hip is thrusting forward and down or "under" in concert with my left shoulder moving up, and thus pushing my left hip *laterally* toward the target. At another time, depending on the state of my game or metabolism, I might think of my left hip thrusting forward in concert with my right shoulder coming down, and thus *pulling* my right hip forward and down or "under." Until pretty late in the forward swing—I'd guess up to about the point where my hands reach hip height—I want to feel that both hips are moving *laterally* toward the target, not turning to the left.

At this stage about 70 percent of my weight will have moved onto the *inside* edge of my left foot. The remainder will be on the inside edge of my right foot, the heel of which will still be on the ground. My right foot is continuing to thrust my legs and my flexed knees *laterally* toward the target, but I'm not really conscious of this right-foot/knee action. A greater concern is keeping both knees roughly level with each other—not letting the right knee collapse forward and thereby pull my whole right side forward.

My wrists at this hip-high point remain fully hinged: The clubhead is still a long way behind my hands—pictures show the shaft has yet to pass vertical. But I have no sensation in my hands and arms. They are relaxed, passive, "free agents." At no point do I consciously try to accelerate or decelerate them; I simply let whatever is happening to them go on happening. Of course, I know that by now my hands and arms will be swinging the club very fast—probably

RIGHT-KNEE BEHAVIOR

How your right knee behaves late in the downswing is an important point to watch. Although it should join the left knee in thrusting laterally toward the target and thus move *forward* of its address position, the right kneecap should still pretty much "look" at the ball through impact.

The knee will swing around to face the target after impact, as the momentum of the through-swing pulls your right heel up. But if your right knee swings around too soon, it can easily pull your right side forward "over" the shot.

bringing it to its maximum rate of acceleration. But I will be oblivious of them as contributors to speed or power. They will be working automatically as a hinged lever, entirely as a result of other forces being exerted in the rest of my body.

IMPACT ZONE. I am now near to, or actually entering, the "hitting area," which I feel begins at the point where centrifugal force on the clubhead becomes so great that it forces the wrists to uncock—the hinge in the lever to straighten. Now I begin to feel that my hips, from moving laterally in the same forward direction as my knees, are beginning to turn to the left of the target.

RIGHT-ARM ACTION

In most good golf swings the right arm is slightly bent and the right elbow pointing down, not out, at impact. Otherwise there's a danger that the right side will grab control of the swing, invariably with dire results.

Past impact, however, the right arm does straighten and extend toward the target. To me, the movement feels very similar to that used in bowling or in pitching a softball. It's a "sweeping through" motion from which I get the feeling I could reach out and retrieve the flying ball with my right hand.

To make room for the arms to swing the club freely past the body and out toward the target, the golfer must synchronize a smooth turning of his hips toward the target with his targetward leg motion. The faster he makes this hip turn, the later the club will be "released" by his hands and wrists, and thus the greater will be his chance of fading, or slicing, the shot. The slower the golfer's hips turn, the faster his hands and wrists will "release" the club, increasing his chance of drawing, or hooking, the shot.

This turning of the hips—a natural reaction to their turning on my backswing—is fairly pronounced in my game and can be clearly seen in sequence photographs. The purpose of their turning leftward, of course, is to clear a path for my arms to swing past my body. This "clearing" is something I almost always "feel" happen, even though I may not be consciously thinking about it. The more I want to fade the ball, the earlier the hip turn occurs; the more I want to draw the ball, the later it happens.

FIRMING UP THE LEFT SIDE

Collapsing the left side at impact is a common fault of middle- and high-handicap golfers. The body sags at the waist, the left arm crumples, and the left knee goes either sloppy or stiff. These hideous moves largely result from an "out and over" attack on the ball by the right side.

The right side must stay "under" the left side through impact. For it to do so, the left side must provide resistance: it must be firm, extended, resilient. I achieve this left-side resistance through a feeling of stretching from my left foot to the tip of my left shoulder—*without, let me add, straightening my left knee.*

Keeping the weight on the *inside* of the left foot through impact is also fine insurance against collapsing the left side. This takes strong ankles and practice, but it's worth working at if you're a "crumpler."

At this very late juncture in the downswing I have a pronounced feeling of firming up, or stretching, in my left leg and side—the result of the upward movement of my left shoulder and the corollary "bowing in" of my right side. Despite this left-side stretching action, both my knees remain flexed and resilient, neither straightening nor stiffening at any point prior to impact.

IMPACT.   By now the "lever is unhinging" as my wrists and right arm start to straighten. The clubhead, fully "released," is whipping toward the ball at maximum speed.

My preplanning for this critical moment will have centered on four factors: 1. Keeping my head where it's been all along—behind the ball. 2. Swinging the clubhead *through* the ball toward the target—not *to* the ball. 3. Keeping my left arm straight and traveling directly toward the target. 4. Avoiding any independent turning or twisting of the club with my hands and wrists.

And at impact itself? Well, I am still accelerating, still *hitting*. I am "down" on the shot. I am trying to deliver the clubhead solidly and accurately to the ball. As soon as the club meets the ball, I will know by "feel" exactly where it's gone—whether all I've just described has worked or not.

CHAPTER 6

The Full-Shot Swing: Following Through

Whatever you do after the ball leaves the clubhead isn't going to influence the shot one way or another. Nevertheless, I believe it is as important to have as clear a mental concept of the follow-through as of the takeaway, backswing, and forward swing.

A writer working on a mystery story provides a good parallel. Having the end plotted helps him to formulate the beginning and the middle. By serving as his final goal, the follow-through helps the golfer formulate and direct his earlier actions.

Another benefit of follow-through awareness, which I believe may be overlooked in teaching, is that it eliminates—or at least diminishes—"ball consciousness." By focusing his mind on what he will do after impact, the golfer betters his chances of hitting *through* the ball, not *to* it. Indeed, this is so true in my own case that follow-through "pictures" are frequently uppermost in my mind during practice and even, sometimes, during tournament play.

What are these pictures? Well, as with the other phases of the swing, let's try to break them down for individual examination. Again, we'll work from the bottom up.

FEET.   By the time I reach impact on a full shot, I feel that most of my weight is on the *inside* of my left foot. As the ball is being struck, my left ankle rolls and thereby shifts this weight to the outer edge of the foot (if this happened before impact, my left knee would lose its firmness, sag forward, and thereby throw me too far "ahead" of the ball).

SHORTER CLUBS REQUIRE SHORTER FOLLOW-THROUGH

Bear in mind that the shorter the club, the shorter the backswing, thus the shorter the follow-through. There's no need to drop the wedge down your back at the completion of the swing, as you might the driver.

The best policy here is to be natural. Let the club stop at whatever point in the follow-through it runs out of momentum. If you try for a very big follow-through with a short club, there's a chance you'll program a very big backswing and perhaps an overswing that will cost you control.

At impact, the weight remaining on my right foot is very much on its inside edge, and predominantly toward the toe. Ideally, my right heel is just starting to leave the ground; the right leg's thrusting action is facilitated by an inward rolling of the ankle rather than a lifting of the heel.

As the follow-through progresses, however, my right heel will rise until the foot is vertical and I am balanced on its toes. I never want my right foot to keel over beyond vertical toward the target line. If it does, I will almost certainly have swung my right side "around," not "under."

By now, the outward rolling of my left ankle will have thrown a high proportion of my weight onto the outside edge of my left foot. However, I swing so hard with the driver that at the very end of the follow-through I experience a sort of involuntary "recoil." The effect of this is to rock a lot of my weight quickly back onto my right foot, and to replant my left foot solidly on the ground.

LEGS.　Once my hips have started to turn in the forward swing and my left leg has "firmed up," it stays firm as I swing through the ball and beyond. The left leg must obviously turn and pivot backward a little, to facilitate the turning of the hips to the left of the target. But I have the feeling that the left leg is anchored: a strong brace against both the hit and the momentum of the follow-through.

The follow-through momentum, of course, pulls my right leg increasingly toward the target: By the time my hands reach shoulder height on the through swing, my right knee is forward of the ball's address position.

HIPS.   Once my hips have started to turn to the left of the target late in the downswing, they continue to move in that direction until, at the completion of the follow-through, they face the target. Occasionally, on a full drive, they'll turn even farther around than that, but this is an undesirable characteristic in that it can mean I've swung my right shoulder "over" rather than "under." At the finish of a good swing my right hip is a little lower than my left, again indicating a "down and through" rather than an "over and around" shoulder turn.

HANDS, WRISTS, ARMS, AND CLUB.   At impact, ideally, the back of my left hand faces the target, and my left arm and the club form a straight line. Thus my left hand and arm are slightly ahead of the ball. The feeling I want thereafter is that this whole hand-wrist-arm-club unit continues to swing out toward the target for as long as possible with the minimum amount of disturbance to its impact "geometry." There is a straightening of the right arm just past impact, but no breaking down of the left arm at the wrist or elbow. And there is no independent rolling, turning, or twisting of my hands, wrists, or forearms until the momentum of the club, combined with my turning body, forces the entire unit to turn and swing to the left of the target line. In other words, I seek the minimum manipulation or collapse or deviation from line of the entire hand-wrist-arm-club unit.

As the follow-through progresses, of course, the whole unit is forced to swing "inside" the target line, because it must follow the turning of my hips and shoulders. But I strive right to the end of the follow-through to swing my arms and the club "out and up," not "over and around." In other words, I strive for a full finish, with my hands high over my left shoulder.

SHOULDERS.   At impact my left shoulder is moving up and around, my right shoulder down and around. This action simply continues as dictated by the momentum of the club, until, at the completion of the swing, my right shoulder has been pulled past my chin, and my left shoulder back behind my head. On a good swing, the left shoulder will be higher than the right, indicating a "down and under" rather than an "over and around" swing plane.

Ideally, the plane of my follow-through shoulder turn will pretty much match the plane of my backswing shoulder turn. If the follow-through plane has become flatter, I will have swung "over" the shot. If it has become even more upright, I will most likely have blocked myself by swinging too much "under."

Although generally the good golfer's downswing shoulder plane is naturally a shade flatter than his backswing plane, consciously attempting to make the planes identical can cure some ugly swing faults for many players. For example, a downswing plane that is too flat relative to the backswing plane is a sure sign of swinging "over" the ball. Conversely, too steep a downswing plane compared with the backswing plane often creates a "blocking" action of the hands and arms through the ball.

HEAD.   For as long as possible into the follow-through my head stays where it was at address, with my chin turned to the right so that I look at the ball's original position through my left eye. I make a conscious effort to "stay down" on the shot by keeping my chin pointing behind the ball, resisting the club's momentum to make my head swivel toward the target. Photos indicate that

KEEP ON ACCELERATING

I think it pays to have the feeling that you are accelerating the club through the ball and out on into the follow-through, even though this may not actually happen—your clubhead may actually reach its highest velocity a foot or two *before* impact.

The danger is that, if you don't think of accelerating through impact, you'll probably decelerate a lot earlier.

my head starts to swivel targetward only when my hands are about hip high. At no point do I let my head rise "up" to look at the ball. Rather, I "trace" the ball's flight path by swiveling my head along the target line, with my eyes hugging the ground, until finally I sort of peer at the ball from behind my right arm and shoulder.

There it is then. The concepts, the mechanics, and the "feels" of one man's golf swing. A lot of words for an event that takes less than two seconds to execute. But in describing my full golf swing I've tried to be as informative and detailed as possible, and all I hope is that something within these chapters has an enlightening, rather than a confusing, effect on *your* golf game!

Now, finally, on the subject of full-swing mechanics, I want to make what I believe are two very important points for golfers who may be looking for shot-making improvement via this book.

The first concerns the influences of my physique on the way I play golf. Through nature's kind auspices and a lifetime of athletic activity, I have very strong legs, and I use them to great effect in my golf swing—probably as much as any golfer on tour. On the other hand, I have relatively weak hands and arms, and I use them passively throughout the swing, largely as connecting rods to the club.

The point I want to stress yet one more time is that if my legs were weaker and my hands and arms stronger, there's a probability I should have had to modify their respective roles. I might feel a different emphasis at certain points in the swing; I might even play a different way entirely. Please keep that in mind if you decide to give the Jack Nicklaus system a try, but don't happen to have my kind of physical makeup.

The other point I want to make brings us back to that deathless subject of golfing debate, "method." Although I wish it weren't the case, it is probably inevitable that some of the material in this book will be used in attempts to prove or disprove theoretical points about the golf swing—particularly, unless I miss my guess, in the "body vs. hands" debate.

Well, as the foregoing must conclusively prove, the emphasis in my game is on body action. In fact, if it were on hand action I have the feeling I'd still be selling insurance and beating it around Scioto for two-dollar Nassau Saturday mornings. I don't mean to say that my hands play no part in hitting a golf ball. They most certainly *do*. But in my case, unlike that of the predominantly "hands" player, the hands function as a *result,* not as a *determinant,* of body action.

This was another interesting point that arose in the discussion with British teaching ace John Jacobs that I mentioned some chapters earlier. John finds that many golfers who have read instructional books and/or studied swing-sequence photographs, tend to overemphasize body action at the expense of hand or arm action. He blames this overemphasis on two factors. First, he says, modern playing professionals who write about their games nearly all emphasize body action because their hands and arms work automatically. Second, he feels the stop-action camera's depiction of the good golfer's super-delayed hand or wrist release on the forward swing makes it look like the hands and arms are being deliberately restrained during the downswing.

Jacobs claims these two factors cause a lot of club golfers to try to take

FOLLOWING THROUGH FOR ACCURACY

I think a greater feeling of "extension" through the ball would help many golfers with directional problems.

The feeling I seek when I am trying to be particularly accurate is one of keeping the ball on the clubface a long time; sort of riding the club out after the ball—"chasing" it, so to speak. Although it's obviously physically impossible actually to accomplish this, I get the feeling that I am when I stay well down on the shot and make an especially low and extended follow-through.

A RIGHT-FOOT SWING INDICATOR

The alignment of the right foot at the finish of the swing tells you a lot about the swing itself.

If your right foot is roughly vertical after you have gone up onto its toes, you'll most likely have swung nicely "under" yourself. But if your right heel leans over toward the target line a good deal, you'll more than likely have swung "around" yourself.

their hands and wrists out of the swing entirely. In his words to me: "Many golfers try to force themselves into the 'late hit' position shown in sequence pictures of people like you, Jack, by deliberately restraining the release of the clubhead on the way down—by holding back with their hands, wrists, and arms."

To effect a cure, Jacobs finds that he has to accent a free, fast arm-swing —or even, in the worst cases, a temporary feeling by the pupil that he's "throwing" the clubhead into the ball from the top.

Well, John asked me for an opinion on this matter, and what I told him was this. In my view, it is impossible to "release" too early with the hands, wrists, and arms *so long as the legs and hips have worked ahead of them and the left hand holds onto the club firmly*. I think I actually said the following: "When I move my legs and left side correctly starting down, I can hit as hard as I like from the top of the swing—really throw the clubhead into the ball with everything I've got. So long as my left hand stays in control of the club, I'll hit good shots. In fact, that's just how I hit my biggest drives."

I bring this point up, in closing the section on full-swing mechanics, because I'd like you to keep it in mind if you ever decide to give the Nicklaus-type swing a serious trial. Remember, please, that the trick is *not* consciously to hold back with your hands, wrists, and arms—ever. The trick is to use your body to make those components work in the right direction at the right time. But work they certainly must, unless you'll be content to play your approach shots before everyone else the rest of your golfing days.

CHAPTER 7

Tempo + Rhythm = Timing

Tempo, rhythm, timing. Very popular words in golf. Very important factors in the golf swing. But what do they actually mean?

To me, tempo denotes the over-all *pace* of the swing; its rate of speed; elapsed time from forward press to end of follow-through. Rhythm describes the *texture* of the swing; the variations of speed within the over-all pace. Timing I regard as the way all the separate motions *flow* together. It is the product of tempo and rhythm, the result of the marriage between pace and flow. If the motions meld in a way that produces maximum clubhead speed at impact, the timing is proper.

Where tempo is concerned, I've never really been able to decide which is the chicken and which is the egg. Does sound swing technique promote good tempo, or does good tempo promote sound swing technique? I suspect the answer is the former: The better your technique, the better your tempo will be. But if you see it the other way around, I'm not going to argue with you.

I'm pretty certain about rhythm, however. I believe it depends very largely on swing technique. For example, you rarely see a player on tour, even one with an unorthodox swing, who doesn't at least swing *rhythmically;* and you very rarely see a high-handicapper who does, however good the mechanics of his game might appear to be. I have to believe that the better the rhythm, the better the meld of all the swing's mechanical parts, the better timed will be the shot.

There can be no doubt that a golfer's tempo—how fast or slow he swings over-all—is related to his personality. Just thinking about my playing partners on tour from week to week is enough to convince me that the fast-moving, impatient, highly strung kind of guy will naturally swing faster than the slow-moving, easy-going, more phlegmatic type of fellow. I think this is something every golfer just has to live with. If by nature you do things quickly, or slowly, you're going to swing the golf club basically the same way. Forcing yourself to an opposite extreme is rarely going to work because it's too contrary to your basic instincts or impulses—especially when you are under competitive pressure.

I always like to look back into time for pointers on these indeterminate matters, but unfortunately golf history doesn't provide much help in this case. There have been as many fast swingers as slow swingers among the great players, although I rather think the relatively slower swingers have lasted longer: Julius Boros, Sam Snead, and Tommy Bolt are examples. But then there is old greased lightning himself, Arnold Palmer. He rather refutes that, doesn't he?

I'd describe my own swing tempo as relatively slow at its best, slow-to-medium at its worst. My father always worked on me to slow it down. No matter how well I happened to play, he'd tell me: "Jack, I don't think you were quite slow and smooth enough out there today." I'd promise to try to do better the next day, because I knew how much he loved to watch me swing

SWINGING WITH FEET TOGETHER IMPROVES TEMPO

A very fine device for improving your tempo, smoothing out your rhythm, and improving your balance is to swing with your feet together, and when I say together I mean actually touching.

Don't hit a ball at first. Start by swinging a five- or six-iron easily backward and forward. Gradually extend the length of the swing as your feeling of smoothness and evenness increases. Then just put a ball in the way of the clubhead's path and go on swinging.

Fifty shots hit like this could do wonders for your tempo and rhythm. This maneuver is also a fine way to start developing a tempo slower than the one you've been playing with.

GOLF MY WAY
Jack Nicklaus

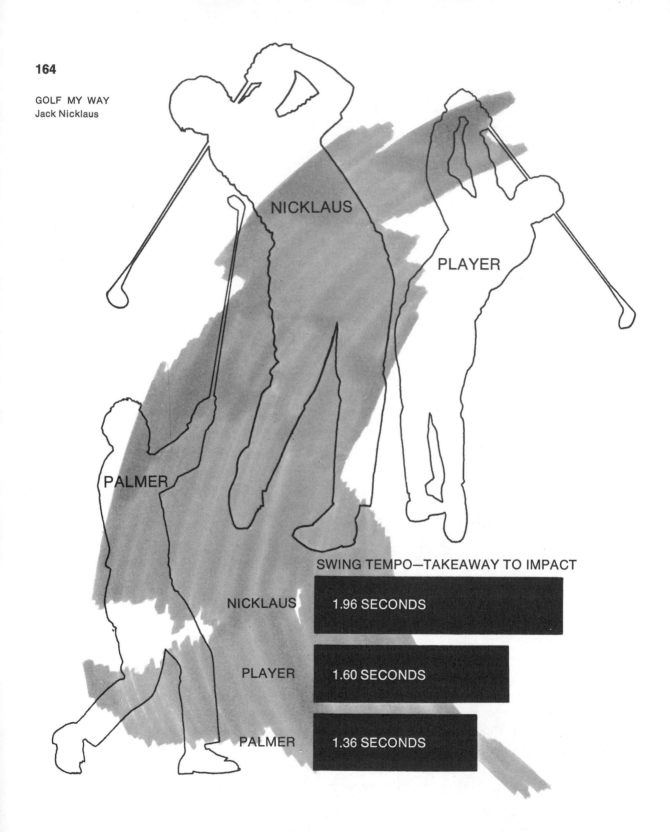

NICKLAUS

PLAYER

PALMER

SWING TEMPO—TAKEAWAY TO IMPACT

NICKLAUS   1.96 SECONDS

PLAYER   1.60 SECONDS

PALMER   1.36 SECONDS

OVER-TIGHT GRIP CAN CAUSE JERKY SWING

Don't confuse a firm grip with too tight a grip. The latter at address can easily force you to swing jerkily, and thus destroy both tempo and rhythm.

Hold the club very lightly at address and firm up your hands a little just before you start back, but don't grab the club in a death grip. Merely allow your hands instinctively to develop the correct amount of pressure needed to control the club at various points in the swing.

on those occasions when it really did seem to him as though I were swinging in slow motion.

One reason I have a relatively slow tempo is that I have a big swing—a very full arc on both sides of the ball. It's tough to swing fast and still keep your balance if you go as far back and as far through as I do. Another reason I'm not normally a fast swinger, in terms of elapsed time, is that I'm not a "hands" player: It simply takes longer to make a golf swing using predominantly your legs and body than it does using predominantly your hands and arms. But I'm sure the chief reason for my slow-to-medium swing tempo is actually my temperament.

I'm fortunate to have the ability to think fairly quickly, and I can often be decisive—too decisive at times, my family and friends tell me! But I'm not really a fast reactor. I'm basically a *deliberate* person. Most of the snap decisions I've made in my life, I've regretted later. Thus, as I've matured, I've learned increasingly to go along with my basic instinct, which is to reason things out and reflect a little before I act; to let myself be deliberate. And I think this has rubbed off on my golf swing, because I believe that my swing tempo now—when I'm playing well—is slower than it's ever been.

I think we also see temperamental characteristics influencing athletes in other sports. In high school basketball I was always a pretty good offensive player—good at driving and faking and getting my shot—because these are deliberate rather than instinctive actions. And I was an excellent foul shooter —I think I led my team in foul shooting every year (even now, when I haven't shot a foul in fifteen years, give me ten warmups and I bet I could make twenty out of twenty-five). Again, deliberation. But as a defensive player—

forget it. I couldn't react quickly enough to the other fellow's moves. He'd be around me and gone while I was still deliberating what he was going to do.

The same thing is true of my tennis today. I react too slowly ever to be as good a player as I'd like to be. Returning a slow shot, say a soft lob, I'm fine. I can think, deliberate on a stroke, and make it happen. But a fast, driving shot will get past me far too often. I'm standing there trying to make a swing, deliberating about the stroke, instead of hitting the ball back instinctively.

But let's get back on the main track. Whether they naturally swing with a fast, medium, or slow tempo, I think a lot of golfers miss out with their spread or distribution of speed—their rhythm—within their over-all tempo.

You will occasionally see a golfer who takes the club back so slowly he looks like he's on TV in a slow-motion replay. You almost expect to hear Byron Nelson or Bob Toski start analyzing the action. Then, suddenly, at the top, the guy turns into a Keystone Cop. All hell breaks loose. There's a flurry of arms and legs, and the club hurtles down like a shaft of lightning. Less often you'll see the opposite act: The golfer whips the club back like there was no tomorrow and then, because he's used up so much energy getting it to the top, he sort of drops or flops it on the ball.

I'm exaggerating, of course, but to make an often overlooked point: The

"COMPLETE THE BACKSWING"

"Complete the backswing" is one of the best mental pictures I know to develop proper tempo and consistent rhythm.

Especially in bad weather, or when you're faced with a particularly difficult shot, or when you are under pressure for any reason, it's easy to "start down before you've gone up." This is particularly true for the short-swinging golfer.

At moments like this, I concentrate on swinging my left shoulder well under my chin, and my hands well above my head, before starting to swing down. Invariably I swing more evenly and smoothly as a result.

If your swing is naturally on the short side, think less of high hands and more of hip turn. This will have much the same effect.

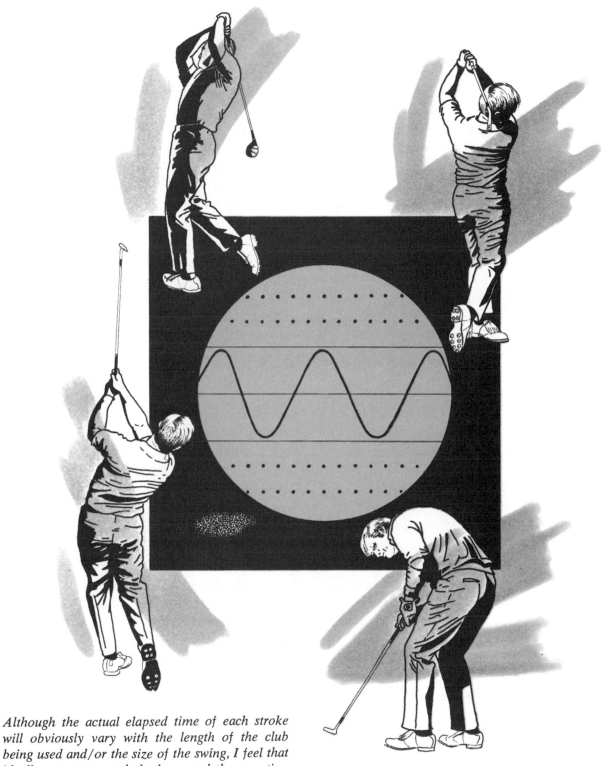

Although the actual elapsed time of each stroke will obviously vary with the length of the club being used and/or the size of the swing, I feel that ideally my tempo and rhythm—and thus my timing—are identical irrespective of whether I'm using a driver, a putter, or any of the twelve clubs in between.

better the rhythm of the swing the better the swing is likely to work, irrespective of whether its over-all tempo is slow, medium, or fast.

This is certainly true of my golf. Regardless of what length or type of shot I want to play, the closer I *feel* that I match the speed of my backswing to that of my down-and-through swing, the greater my chance of success. Actually, of course, the speed of the swing's two phases never does match. In a good golf swing the forward swing always happens very much faster than the backswing. But that's really our old friends cause and effect: If you've made the correct backswing motions, the forward swing motions will take care of themselves. The point I'm getting at is not what happens reflexively, but how you program your mind consciously. What happens to me is that, by thinking *"even* rhythm," I best allow the swing's accelerative-decelerative-accelerative-decelerative speed pattern to happen reflexively. If I think "slow back, fast down"—or even "slow back, slow down"—I tend to *force* the action at some point, and thereby will almost certainly disrupt its rhythm.

In mechanical terms, my takeaway rhythm establishes my over-all tempo. As I explained earlier I am a believer in the most deliberate, unhurried start back consistent with swinging rather than maneuvering the club away from the ball. This establishes the mood I want to retain all the way through to the finish: deliberateness, lack of rush or hurry, plenty of time to let the correct moves happen in the correct sequence. But getting the club away in this mood is really only half the battle. The other, and more difficult, half is getting it started down in the same deliberate, unhurried mood; completing the backswing; waiting to feel the tension of the clubhead against the shaft; not thrusting too hard with my legs; not racing down with my hands.

Which brings me to the point of technique that I believe has the highest bearing on rhythm; namely, the hands. They are, I believe, given the slightest opportunity, the Great Destroyer of good timing in the golf swing.

The case against the hands in terms of rhythm and timing doesn't really need much spelling out when you think about what the hands are and what they do. They are the fastest-reacting, fastest-moving external parts of the body except, I suppose, the eyes. You use your hands in everyday living more often and more spontaneously than any of your other limbs—they are naturally hyperactive. And, not least important, as the golfer's only connection with the club, they offer him his greatest sense of security in regard to making contact with the ball.

If you add all that up, what it means is that the hands, if you let them, will totally dominate the golf swing. And, because they can act so much faster and so much more independently than any other part of the body, their worst crime is frequently to force a disastrous change in rhythm. If the hands start the club back, they will tend to *flash* it back. If they've been in charge of taking it back, they will want to bring it down again, *quickly*—often long before the rest of you has moved into a good backswing position. Even if you have started back slowly with a good, one-piece movement, if you let your hands take over at the top, they will most likely try to *flash* the club back to the ball before your legs can go to work. Given even the slightest opportunity, they can become despotic dictators of the swing, and thus the most dangerous threat of all to consistent tempo and smooth rhythm.

What's the answer to this problem? If you're predominantly a "hands"

The hyperactivity of one's hands in everyday life, plus the fact that they are the golfer's only link with his striking implement, often makes them the Great Destroyers of good golf. Nowhere is this more true than at the start of the downswing. Given a ghost of a chance, almost every golfer's hands will start to flash the club down to the ball way before any other part of his anatomy can go to work. My method of keeping these limelight-hoggers backstage until they are automatically called into action in the hitting zone is merely to try to feel that they are not moving any faster on the first half of the forward swing than they were during the final phase of the backswing. When I'm successful, my shots fly farther, because proper pace and sequence of downswing movement accelerate the club to maximum velocity at impact.

"FEEL" THE CLUBHEAD FOR IMPROVED RHYTHM

Feeling the weight of the clubhead against the tension of the shaft helps me to swing rhythmically.

As the backswing progresses I like to feel the clubhead's weight "pulling" my hands and arms back and up. Starting down, I like to feel the weight of the clubhead lagging back—resisting—as my thrusting legs and hips pull my arms and hands down.

When I can "wait" for these feels, I am almost certainly swinging in proper tempo. I am giving myself enough elapsed time to make all the various moves in rhythmical sequence.

player, frankly I don't know. In fact, I think it's because there probably isn't an answer that so many "hands" players are so erratic: hot one day, cold the next. But in my case, as a golfer whose hands play an essentially passive role in the swing, the answer is simply to maintain their passivity; to keep them subservient; to make them followers, not leaders.

Maintaining passive hands is particularly critical, for me, at the beginning of my forward swing. This is where my hands will leap into a starring role and in a flash destroy the even rhythm I am trying to maintain—and with it, inevitably, the shot. My device for keeping them backstage is, however, simple. I merely try to feel that they are not moving any faster on the first half of my forward swing than they were during the latter half of my backswing. This way I can almost always keep them under control; doing the job I want them to do, rather than the job they instinctively want to do. Then, invariably, the over-all tempo of my swing will match the mood of my takeaway.

Now, what about timing—the putting together of all the moving swing parts into a smooth-flowing whole? Here I'm going to have to be brief, because I think good timing derives from confidence, and I *know* that confidence derives only from efficient swing mechanics. To improve your timing, you must work on the basics of your swing. The more you improve your fundamentals of grip, setup, takeaway, and change-over from back to forward swing, the better your timing will become.

To my mind, Lee Trevino provides the classic example of this principle.

His swing may look unorthodox, but mechanically it is both immensely efficient and deeply "grooved." He has developed a set of motions that get the
job done, framed them within a beautifully rhythmical pattern of movement
and, through endless practice, made the whole package wonderfully repetitive.
Thus he now has superb timing—perhaps the finest on tour. Ben Hogan,
although his tempo was faster than Trevino's, is another fine example of good
rhythm and excellent timing growing out of mechanical excellence. Of the
slow-tempo swingers, Sam Snead unquestionably provides the indelible example of fine timing born of efficient mechanics and smooth rhythm.

In the end, excellent timing—the *quality,* one might say, of delivering
the club's maximum momentum to the ball—is simply the product of tempo
and rhythm. To have good "timing," you must first have a good tempo: a
pace of swing at which you can best swing efficiently and consistently. Then
you must have good rhythm, which means that the speed of each portion of
your swing must blend into a smooth, effective whole. To achieve that, the
mechanics of your swing must be sound, reciprocating, and mutually com-
patible.

Given both of these—tempo and rhythm—you will develop good "timing." All your various moves will work together to produce solid contact time
after time—the end goal of any serious golfer. But, like all good things, it isn't
easily earned.

CHAPTER 8

Power

OFF THE TEE

People often ask me: "What was the longest drive you ever hit?" When I tell them I don't know, I'm not being modest. I have a good memory, good recall of my golf career, but I measure success in scores, not yardages. In fact, even that isn't strictly true, because scores mean far less to me than what they actually achieve. I'm not record conscious; I'm *win* conscious. Anytime I come to the last hole of a major championship needing a par to win and a birdie to break the tournament record, I'll play safe for the par. I was just as happy to win the 1972 Masters with 286 as I was the 1965 Masters with 271.

The shots that stick in my mind are not drives, but the approaches, recoveries, and putts that had significant effect on the outcome of tournaments that were particularly important to me. I could describe such shots, good and bad, all day, but drives fade quickly from my mind. Don't misunderstand me. It gives me as big a thrill as the next guy to hit a hard, solid drive, and in the sense that one must generally put the ball in play up to fourteen times per round with the driver, I regard it as the most important club in the bag. But distance is usually much less of a factor in my mind than giving myself the most advantageous position for the ensuing shot.

Please understand that I am talking here aesthetically. No one more deeply appreciates the value of distance in golf—or his own talent for it—than I. But I also happen to believe that distance isn't as big a factor in professional tournament golf as the average fan likes to make out. If it were, the longest hitters would win every week. The record shows that they actually win less often than many shorter but straighter hitters.

Nor do the biggest-hitting professionals actually drive the ball as far as many fans seem to think they do. Constantly at tournaments you'll hear comments like: "Wow! I bet he busted that ball 320 yards!" Maybe downwind, downhill, on dried-out fairways, he did. But most of the time he didn't— any more than the handicap player who drives from the fronts of the tees at his home club and then relates his distance to what the blue-tee card indicates as the distance. He isn't hitting the consistent 250 he likes to think he does.

For quite a number of years in the U. S. Open, the United States Golf Association has computed the lengths of all drives played on a couple of representative holes. A few years ago, IBM compiled similar distance statistics over the course of 22,700 PGA tour rounds. Here is what those studies show: The average *carry* of the drive in professional tournament play is 238 yards; the average total driving distance (carry and run) is 247 yards. Not quite as sensational as it looks from outside the ropes, right?

How do I compare with this? Well, I know that a lot of the people who watch me out on tour think I hit every drive at least 300 yards. The facts are that I *occasionally* drive 300 yards or more—but only when I have a tailwind, or a lot of run on the ball, or both. When I'm swinging well, my average drive carries about 260 yards on a windless summer day. To fly the ball 270 yards through the air, I really have to jump out of my socks. I doubt if I could *ever* carry the U.S.-size ball more than 280 yards in still air at sea level. I did carry over 300 yards a few times, in still air, while practicing for the 1971 World Cup at Palm Beach Gardens, Florida, but that was with some incredibly "hot" Australian-made, British-size balls.

One hole in particular out on tour—the eighteenth at a course I had a hand in designing, Harbour Town, on Hilton Head Island, South Carolina— indicates the truth about distance in pro golf about as well as anything I can think of. The ideal drive from the tee used in the annual Heritage Classic will carry 230 yards across a lagoon to a landing spot on a sort of peninsula fairway. It doesn't actually look that far, and most of the pros stand up to the drive with normal confidence when they first play the hole. But the fact is that many of them can't carry to that spot unless they hit their absolutely best shot. In my own case, I know if I mishit the shot by much—catch it a little thin, for instance—I won't make it either.

Another question I'm often asked by friends and fans is: "How do you feel when you're outdriven?" Well—to be immodest, I suppose—until recently

"COORDINATE" YOUR DRIVER TO YOUR SWING STYLE

A highly technical but important distance factor is the compatibility of a golfer's driver to his swing style.

I like to get my distance through the air, thus I must hit the ball relatively high. To help achieve this I use a driver that is comparatively "soft" (S shaft) in relation to how hard I swing, yet doesn't have a great degree of loft (10 degrees). I feel that this shaft, by virtue of the fact that it flexes the clubhead forward just before impact, gives me a little extra speed through the ball. At the same time, the forward flexing increases the effective loft of the clubface by a degree or two, helping me to hit the ball high.

On a couple of occasions when I've anticipated strong winds—at the British Open, for example—I've experimented with an X-shafted driver. The stiffer shaft reduces the clubhead's pre-impact "forward kick"; thus with it I hit the ball lower. But because I'm getting less help from the shaft, I have to swing a little harder with such a club to achieve the distance I get with the S-shafted driver. Thus, because the harder swing jeopardizes my tempo, I've rarely used the X-shafted driver in actual tournament play.

Once you have a reasonably sound swing, I believe it might be worth your while to experiment with various driver formulas. The objective is to find a club that jives with your swing tempo, that gives you maximum distance and the trajectory you desire on most of your tee shots without necessitating a change in swing tempo.

I really hadn't been consistently outdriven by anyone hitting the ball straight (foul balls don't count) in quite a long time. But at the 1972 British Open at Muirfield I played several practice rounds with Tom Weiskopf; I feel that no one on tour has more natural golfing talent than he. I wasn't playing particularly well and Tom was playing superbly: He'd been shooting in the mid-sixties every day. On just about every par-5 and long par-4 hole that day,

Tom knocked it a good 20 yards past me—and dead in the center of the fairway. I realized, as the round progressed, that even if I'd been playing well I couldn't have matched him. And, candidly, I found it very demoralizing. Of course, it was only practice and therefore not as bad as it would have been in the championship proper. But this experience gave me a very good insight into how little Gary Player must have felt when Arnold Palmer and I were enjoying a slugging contest in those head-to-head TV matches the three of us played some years back. No wonder Gary ate all those raisins and did all those pushups.

What I have learned—even as a relatively long hitter—is that, first, there'll always be someone who can knock it past you occasionally; and, second, that power becomes a real asset only in ratio to your ability to hit straight as well as long.

I believe this latter point is an important one that many club golfers overlook. Everybody would like more distance; I've never met a guy yet, pro or amateur, who wouldn't. That's human nature. But if your aim is to win golf matches rather than *machismo* contests, you'd better decide whether more distance is really worth the price.

For example, I've just indicated that my average carry is maybe 260 yards, but that I can get 270 without tearing too many muscles. Why don't I go for 270 all the time? Because I can hit 260 and know where the ball is going—*I can place it accurately at that distance*. At 270 I not only cannot place the ball as accurately, but I am also aware that the greater the distance the ball does go, the more any error in its direction will be magnified. Thus, I'll generally settle for 260 on the fairway rather than 270 in the rhubarb. And even if I were a shorter hitter I believe I'd still settle for the fairway, so long as there was a club in my bag that would get me home on most par-4s.

I'm very aware that this philosophy is easier to live with for a fellow who carries 260 yards consistently than it is for a fellow who hits 190 on average and wants to be a low-handicap player. Obviously, distance to him must seem like the key to the pearly gates. If he's a beginner or a youngster I say go ahead, swing as hard as you like, move it out there first and worry about where it goes later. But if he's an established golfer, with set habits and swing patterns, I'd encourage him to seek more clubhead speed—and thus more distance —only if he can learn to control the extra clout. If he can't, if more distance means greater wildness in the long run, then I'd suggest he learn to live with the length of drive he can control and seek improvement in other areas of his game.

Much earlier in this book we looked at my concept of the source of power.

You'll probably remember that the formula was "leverage = centrifugal force = clubhead speed = distance." Having indicated as best I can how I apply that formula when describing my swing, I'm not going to get into "mechanics" again here. There is, however, one other factor relating to distance that does deserve more attention in these pages.

For an average-size guy (5 feet 11½ inches, 185 pounds, size 42 regular coat), I generate considerable clubhead speed. But I also hit the ball very squarely, very *true*—at least on my better shots. In technical terms the clubhead is traveling on a very precise path and the clubface is looking in a very specific direction at the moment of impact. If this were not the case, I could swing the clubhead at twice the speed I do and still not be able to get home in 2 on a 400-yard par-4.

The point I want to make here is that there are really *two* ways of increasing your distance. You can learn to swing the clubhead *faster*. Or you can learn to deliver it to the ball more *accurately*. Which you choose, I suggest, must depend on your physical makeup, age, present level of skill, and other such personal factors. The best advice I can offer has to be general. If you swing slowly or easily, but think you could swing the clubhead faster while still making square contact with the ball, then that's your way to go. If you swing

MAXIMIZE YOUR GREATEST ASSETS

I think strong legs are the greatest asset a golfer can have in terms of producing power, and in that sense I'm very fortunate. But if you're not similarly blessed, don't give up the game. Look for your own best assets and try to find a way to play that maximizes them.

Arnold Palmer is the perfect example of a golfer who uses what he's got to maximum effect. Arnie's back, shoulders, and arms are stronger than his legs, and he has built a swing that predominantly uses those power sources.

Chi Chi Rodriguez is another example. Like a lot of very small but wiry people, Chi Chi can move very fast. Thus he uses speed of movement rather than muscular strength to generate his sometimes quite-awesome distance off the tee.

The three elements of power: 1, clubhead speed; 2, on-line delivery of clubhead relative to target line; 3, square impacting of clubface on ball. Distance is diminished anytime any one of these three elements is missing.

TEEING THE BALL FOR DISTANCE

I tee the ball fairly high for a normal drive, usually so that the center of the ball is about opposite the top edge of the clubface. This helps me to hit the ball high by catching it either exactly at the bottom of the swing arc or very slightly on the upswing.

I believe teeing the ball low with the driver can easily rob you of distance by making you "hit down" on the ball, rather than sweeping through it. The steeper the angle of attack with the driver, the more glancing the blow (in a downward direction); thus the greater the backspin you'll impart. You need some backspin on every shot to get the ball in the air, but with the driver too much backspin will rob you of both carry and roll. The way to minimize backspin is to sweep the club through the ball on a relatively level path. It is easiest to do this and still avoid catching the ground when the ball is teed high.

the clubhead fast already but don't deliver it accurately, then it is control you need to work on, not speed. But I do believe that just deciding in your own mind exactly which "medicine" you need most will help you add some distance almost immediately.

I want to round out these thoughts on distance by offering you some help with your long-iron play, an important—and often neglected—department of power golf. But before doing so, there's one more point I'd like to touch on relating to power generally.

It's true, unfortunately, that the more desperately you try to hit the ball farther, the worse your chance of doing so becomes. *Determination,* leading to study, intelligent experiment, and practice, can certainly add distance to your shots. *Desperation,* leading to mental and physical fury, won't—ever. Mental fury simply destroys reason, and if there is a game in the world that demands reason, it is a game like golf, where you have to self-ignite; to start from cold; where the action must be deliberate, not reactive. Physical fury certainly creates muscular force, but muscular force per se does not produce clubhead speed. If it did, the world's strongest men would hit the ball farthest; instead, I've found they often hit it like Aunt Ethel.

What I'm trying to say is that you can't "muscle" the ball farther. Power in the strength sense leads to power in the yardage sense only when it's applied with a well-timed *swing*. Not a bash, or a thump, or a punch, or a swat, or a swipe, or a belt, but a *swing*. Never lose sight of this fact if you decide to go in search of more distance. Any time you don't *swing* the club, you must be "putting" or "placing" or "taking" it someplace—in other words, forcing it, over-controlling it. Your muscles must be hard, tight, tense, instead of loose, relaxed, supple. Only with extreme luck will you be able to direct the club to the ball accurately in that condition. And even if you get lucky in the accuracy stakes, you're never going to propel the club through the ball as fast with muscular force as you could with a well-timed *swing*.

INTO THE GREEN

A couple of years ago a magazine writer asked me what I thought was my biggest advantage over other players on tour. My first answer was that, if I had any particular advantage, it was probably my ability to hit a six-iron over a tree that most fellows would need a nine-iron to clear. Then I reflected a moment and told him—a little immodestly, I'm afraid—"No, that's not it. My advantage is being able to hit a one-iron over a tree that other fellows would need a six-iron to clear."

One chap who I know would agree that my long-iron game sometimes gives me an edge is Gary Player. I remember him telling the press at a tournament a few years ago: "Thit fellow Nicklaus is incridible. Just *in-crid-ible*. Man, he can hit a one-iron so high it would stop on concrete. On *concrete*, I'm telling you, man!"

Gary was exaggerating wildly, of course, but it is true that the ability to hit high long-iron shots is a tremendous asset in golf, particularly on courses that call for long, accurate, soft-landing approaches to firm, dry greens, like those at Augusta National and most of the courses used for the U. S. and British Opens. There have been so many occasions in my career—particularly in major championships—where the ability to pull off this type of shot has made the difference between winning and losing, that I have to regard long-iron play as my strongest suit.

Now, having declared my prejudice for the long irons, I want to let you

A BIG-HIT STANCE ADJUSTMENT

The speed of my forward-swing leg and hip action is the major determinant of how far I'll hit the ball. When I'm really going for a big one, I often make a slight stance adjustment that helps me to speed up my leg thrust and hip turn.

The adjustment is simply to point my left foot more toward the target, say at 40 degrees instead of 30 degrees to the ball-target line. This gives me, in effect, a "running start" in shifting my hips out of the way faster on the forward swing.

If you try this, be sure you start down with your legs. If you don't, the "opened" left-foot position will make it very easy for you to spin your shoulders "over the top."

into a little secret about them. You know all that stuff you've read and heard about how difficult they are to play? Well, I think it's rubbish. Unless you make the two- and three-irons more difficult, by letting them either pysche you out or by swinging them in some contrived or artificial way, they are really no more difficult than the four- and five-irons. And if you can play a two-iron, there's no reason on earth why you shouldn't be able to play a one-iron.

I'm sure that 90 percent of the reason why golfers who are quite competent with every other club in the bag shun the long irons is psychological. They've been hexed. One day, long ago, some golfer copped out. He decided that, because his long irons were a little longer in the shaft than his middle irons, and had a little less loft, and thus *looked* more difficult, they had to *be* more difficult. And he started telling his pals about this great discovery, and they started telling theirs, and all of a sudden the word had flashed around the world: "Long irons are too tough for club golfers. Death to long irons! Long live the baffy!"

If you're sold on this idea, then by all means jump to the next chapter. But if you're ready to wipe the dust off those nice, shiny long sticks, and put all that "impossible" stuff out of your head, then I think we might be able to do your game a little good.

The first thing I'd like you to do is to determine that henceforth you are going to swing your long irons more like you do your three-wood than your wedge. In other words, you're going to stop "hitting down on the ball," and start "sweeping through it." It is true that to get a golf ball lying on the ground airborne it helps to strike it just *before* the clubhead begins its upward arc, so as to apply sufficient backspin to the ball to make it rise. But that doesn't mean you need swing the club *abruptly* downward. With the long irons, the closer you can come to contacting the ball just a fraction of an inch before the clubheads reaches the lowest point in its arc, the better the shots you'll play. You'll get your backspin, but you will also apply all of the loft that the manufacturer built into the clubhead.

I have been told that Harry Vardon was a beautiful long-iron player, and also that he never took a divot with any club in the bag. Usually he'd just neatly shave off a little grass, sometimes not even that. I believe the two go together. On most of my long-iron shots I also try to just nip the top off the grass beneath the ball. Only when I am trying to really "punch" a shot will I take a true divot —grass *and* earth—with a long iron.

To catch the ball the right way, it must be played at the point where the clubhead just reaches the bottom of its arc. For the handicap player this usually means farther forward in relation to his feet than he's been positioning the ball whenever he did dare to try a long-iron shot. And, since sweeping the ball requires that the hands be only *slightly* ahead of it at impact, it's best to put them there at address—not way ahead of the ball, as the thumper-down has probably become used to doing.

To give yourself a little start-up courage, I suggest you first practice the long irons with the ball teed—air has far less resistance than dirt. Get the ball

SWING SMOOTHLY, NOT EASILY

I've always thought the phrase "hit it nice and easy," when a golfer needed a big shot, was dopey advice. "Hit it nice and *smoothly*" sounds much better to me.

You'll never hit the ball very far by thinking of swinging at it easily. A much better mental picture, to me, is one of hitting the ball as hard as possible while still swinging the club rhythmically.

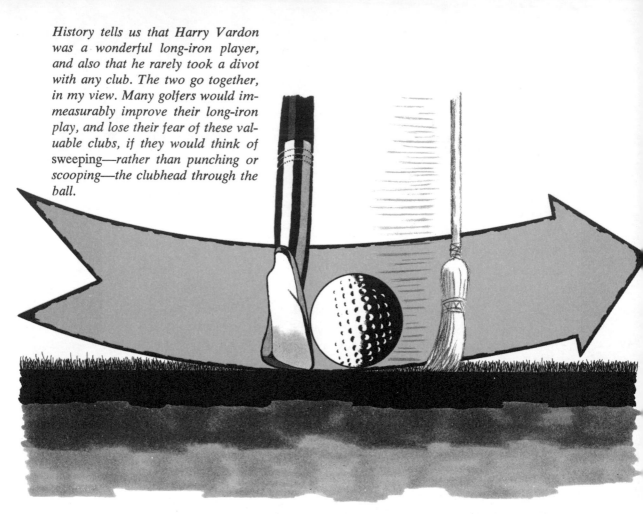

History tells us that Harry Vardon was a wonderful long-iron player, and also that he rarely took a divot with any club. The two go together, in my view. Many golfers would immeasurably improve their long-iron play, and lose their fear of these valuable clubs, if they would think of sweeping—rather than punching or scooping—the clubhead through the ball.

well up in the air. Any time I need a big long-iron carry on a par-3 hole I tee the ball at least half an inch above ground, thus giving myself the best chance of sweeping the ball off the center of the clubface.

Now let's talk about the actual long-iron swing. The worst fault I see among amateurs who do pluck up courage enough to pull out a long iron in a pro-am is a *forced* golf swing. They seem to have a compulsive urge to *muscle* the ball. A fellow might be sailing along merrily, swinging smoothly and hitting the ball solidly, until suddenly he's faced with a shot that calls for, say, the two-iron. He'd really rather hit his four-or five-wood, or choke down on the three-wood, but no, he's playing with the pros. . . . So out comes the two-iron and, with it, a new golf swing. Invariably it is a faster, shorter, and tighter swing—a whole new tempo. And invariably he misses the shot, curses his bravado, and yet again decides to lock those s.o.b.'s in the cellar and throw away the key.

Thus, the biggest hurdle of all in getting reunited with your long irons, if you see anything of yourself in what I've just described, is proving to yourself that these clubs will do an excellent job when swung no harder than you swing a nine-iron. And here's how you do that:

A FAVORITE—AND USEFUL—LONG-IRON SHOT

You often run into long approach shots where it's necessary for the ball to clear bunkers in front of the green, yet not run over it and into even more serious trouble behind.

My favorite shot here—and I believe it's within the capability of anyone who shoots in the low 80s or better—is a high, faded long-iron. I take one more club than I'd seemingly need, move the ball up to my left instep, open the clubface a little more than usual, set up aligned a little farther left than usual, then make my regular swing.

This shot is a primary weapon in my arsenal, and one that I recommend every competent golfer master. If you can't—if your only long-iron shot is a low, hard, fast runner—then you'd usually be better off hitting a softer-landing shot with a lofted wood. But always remember to check the trouble around the green. It's often much worse in back than in front.

Go out on the practice tee and hit a batch of easy nine-irons, trying to capture your ideal tempo and rhythm. When you feel you've got it, pick up your four-iron and hit a dozen shots with exactly the same swing you used with the nine-iron. Now go back to your eight-iron and hit out another batch of pace-setters and rhythm-builders. When those are going good, pick up your three-iron and hit maybe ten shots swinging the same way. Now go back to your seven-iron for another tempo refresher. When the seven-iron swing feels right, grab the two-iron and just keep repeating the seven-iron swing.

I do this sort of thing frequently. It's by far the best discipline I know for proving to myself that long irons don't have to be muscled, and thus for strengthening my friendship with them.

Obviously the 80-to-90 shooter who carries out the kind of program I've suggested here isn't going to become a Harry Vardon overnight. He's going to continue to miss some long-iron shots. Probably many 90-plus shooters should stick to the four- and five-woods until their swing form improves. But most golfers will lose much of their *fear* of the long irons through the kind of practice I've suggested, and build enough confidence through the solid striking that results to use them at least when they are on their games. And that, really, is 99 percent of the battle.

CHAPTER 9

"Trouble"

Along with the physical growth of golf in this country, there seems to have grown a desire to make it a much more predictable game than it was ever intended to be by its founders. I'm not sure I like that tendency, even though predictability in course design and conditions must supposedly improve my career prospects.

Utter predictability in a golf course to me spells blandness, and blandness spells dullness. If I never missed a fairway or green, never got a bad bounce, always got a level lie, I might make a lot more money, but I'd be bored silly doing it. Obviously, the game's greatest thrills lie in planning and executing perfect shots. But I believe that recovering skillfully from poor shots and bad breaks also offers a great challenge, and an additional dimension of satisfaction when you succeed.

"Poor shots, yes," you may say. "But *bad breaks*? Are they fair?" Well, as any Scotsman will tell you, golf was never intended to be a fair game—at least not in the sense that pool or bowling is fair because there the playing conditions are always totally predictable. And there's a story I like about Arnold Palmer that makes the point.

Arnold, it seems, had hit a superb drive on a long par-4 hole in the British Open. He had a three-iron for his second shot, and again he played it magnificently. But just as the ball seemed about to land on the green and head for the cup, it caught a little mound, turned sharply right, and buried under the lip of a deep bunker, leaving him an extremely difficult recovery shot. An American in Arnold's gallery was totally shocked by this turn of fortune, and he couldn't help but expostulate to the Scotsman standing next to him. "That's terrible!" he exclaimed. "That was a *great* shot, and look what happened to it! This course just has to be ridiculously unfair."

The Scotsman gave the American a long, dour look. Then he said: "Tha' mon's a professional gowfer, is he not? Well, then, let's nae bother too much wi' the coorse. Let's see wha' he can do wi' this wee bunker shot."

I can appreciate that this attitude—the acceptance of luck as an integral part of golf—might not appeal too strongly to the golfer who's in trouble more often than he's not. But before you dismiss it out of hand, ask yourself this question: When you get in trouble, either through your own fault or through a bad break, which mental attitude will serve you best: infuriation and self-pity, or a philosophical and positive approach?

I see a lot of bad temper and self-pity on tour, especially on difficult courses. I've been guilty of it myself at times. It's a human enough reaction. As Bob Jones said: "Golf is a game that creates emotions that sometimes cannot be sustained with the club still in one's hand." But even if anger or self-pity are excusable, I still dislike them intensely, in myself even more than in others. The reason is that they are crutches—copouts. You face a situation that you fear you cannot cope with, so you give yourself an excuse for possible failure by getting mad at the course or the injustice you've suffered. The result invariably is that you fail to recover, not only from the one poor swing or unlucky bounce that first upset you, but from all the others that inevitably follow. There have been a dozen golfers on tour in my time who might have been in the superstar class if only they could have better disciplined themselves by developing a deeper understanding and acceptance of golf's true nature—by learning to live with "the rub of the green."

So much for my "trouble" philosophy. To get back to practical solutions, it is my belief that with the right attitude and the right technical knowledge you can almost always avoid turning a trouble situation into a catastrophe on any golf course. The attitude is up to you. To help you on the technical side, I shall describe a few of the shots I have called upon when straying from the straight-and-narrow.

SOME SPECIAL SHOTS

The absolute prerequisite to strong recovery play is a clear understanding of cause and effect: knowing exactly what types of spin—and thus flight—are created by the various combinations of swing path and clubface alignment. If you still have any doubts in this area, may I suggest you restudy Chapter 2 of Part One.

INTENTIONAL SLICE.   I believe the most difficult way to hit an intentional slice is the one most commonly advocated—by altering the grip so that both hands are turned farther than normal to the left on the club, then swinging out to in, across the ball. I believe the easiest way to slice—because it's the soundest way in cause-and-effect terms—is simply to open the clubface at address, aim the feet and shoulders left of target, and then swing normally. The more slice you want, the more you open the clubface and the farther left you align your body. But you never change either your grip or your swing, except in extreme situations. Incidentally, by setting up and swinging thus you add loft to the clubface, so you will require more club than normal.

INTENTIONAL HOOK.   Again, I believe the toughest way to deliberately hook is the one most frequently advocated: turning the hands to the right on the club and swinging in to out. Instead, simply close the clubface at address, align your feet and shoulders right of target at address, and then swing normally. The more hook you want, the more you close the clubface and the farther right you align your body. Because you are delofting the clubface, use less club than normal.

KEEPING THE BALL DOWN.   The easiest way to keep the ball down is to play it farther back at address, then consciously lead the clubhead with the hands through impact. The normal reaction to such a setup and swing is a drawn or hooked shot, which is my preferred shape when the wind is blowing head on or from my left. When the wind is from the right, I'll usually attempt a slow fade by opening the clubface slightly at address and ensuring that my hips move ahead of my hands through impact.

GETTING THE BALL UP.   Extra height with any club is easy to achieve. Simply position the ball a little farther forward at address, open the clubface, allow for a fade, stay well behind the ball in the downswing, and hit hard with the right hand, making sure to work it "under" the left through impact.

HARD PAN.   To achieve decent contact off any kind of hard material, the ball must be met before the descending clubhead touches the ground. The easiest way to achieve such firm "trapping" of the ball is to move it back at address, and when the green is receptive I will usually play the low draw shot that naturally results from this adjustment. But if the green is not receptive to a hard, fast shot I'll often try to "pick" the ball clean by addressing it a little farther forward than normal, so that the club makes contact at the very bottom of the swing rather than while still descending. This is a tough shot to execute perfectly, however, and I believe most handicap golfers will do better by moving the ball back, punching crisply into it, and allowing for draw and run.

LOOSE OBJECTS.   I avoid grounding the club at address in case something I touch might cause the ball to move and cost me a 1-shot penalty. On a full shot I use my normal swing, making whatever setup and arc adjustments are dictated by the severity of the lie. If the loose material is soft, on short shots around the green I will generally swing the same way I do in sand. If the material is hard, I'll normally try to play a chip or a pitch-and-run shot.

THE WATER SHOT.   If no part of the ball is above the surface, it's usually less costly in the long run to drop clear and take the appropriate penalty. If you feel brave, put on your raingear, take a lofted club, and hit steeply down into the water a little farther behind the ball than you think you should, using much the same action that you would employ to "knife" the club under a buried lie in sand.

SHALLOW DEPRESSIONS.   When you want distance from a divot mark or other depression, the rounded sole of a fairway wood will do a better "digging" job for you than the wide blade of a long iron. Open the clubface, set up to expect a fade, then swing firmly on a slightly steeper arc than normal.

DEEP DEPRESSIONS.   This is a tough shot, but it's sometimes worth gambling instead of taking an unplayable-lie penalty. Get down to ball level by accentuating your knee bend. Swing the club up sharply with a quick wrist cock and, if necessary, a bent left arm, then hit straight down into the ball on a similarly steep path. And watch that ball while you do it: This is a potential "head up" shot.

RESTRICTED BACKSWING.   Too many golfers chicken out on shots where they must restrict their backswing due to some overhanging obstacle. Usually these shots are not all that difficult if you will make enough experimental practice backswings to "measure" and get acclimatized to the feel of the restriction. Then forget the obstacle and concentrate on striking the ball cleanly.

BALL AGAINST WALL.   If the ball rests against a wall, fence, tree, or other obstacle but you can swing at it right-handed, you have a shot. Simply close the clubface acutely and make your normal swing. In other words, hit a deliberate hook that will curve toward the target. The closed clubface will cause the ball to fly low and run far, so club yourself accordingly.

PLAYING LEFT-HANDED.   This can sometimes be useful when you can't get at a ball right-handed—as, for example, when its lying close to a tree. But if the lie is poor, or other circumstances indicate you have only a remote chance of moving the ball to a better location by swinging at it left-handed, it's usually less costly to accept an unplayable-lie penalty. To play a left-handed shot, I reverse my grip—left hand below right—and turn the club over so that I hit the ball with its face, not its back. The trick then is to feel out the left-handed action with a number of practice swings, and, on the real thing, to swing as smoothly and slowly as possible. I prefer the five-, six-, and seven-irons for this shot because they offer a generous amount of clubface when reversed. But plan for the ball to hook sharply left off the slanted clubface.

ODD ANGLES

UPHILL LIE.   If you tilt yourself to the right at address so that you stand perpendicular to the slope you will, in effect, give yourself a flat lie. If you then swing the club normally, its arc will follow the slope, going back low and rising coming through. Avoid swaying down the slope on the backswing by restricting your body action a little; use more armswing and less hip turn. This will also offset the tendency to fall onto the back foot during the forward swing. The ball will fly higher and thus shorter than usual, so club yourself accordingly. If the slope is so severe that you are almost certain to lose balance, allow for a pulled shot.

DOWNHILL LIE.   Again, tilt yourself perpendicular to the slope, then swing normally so that the club arc follows the slope back and through. To prevent falling forward, put most of your weight on your back foot at address and keep it there throughout the swing. Accenting arm and wrist action over body turn will again help you to maintain balance. It may also help in preserving balance if you move the ball back a little and open your stance at address. You have to really "stay down" on this shot, chasing the clubhead out after the ball through impact. The ball will tend to fly lower and thus travel farther than normal, so club appropriately. If the slope is so severe that you are bound to lose balance, allow for a pushed shot.

BALL ABOVE FEET.   Because the ball is raised, stand more erect than normal and choke down on the club. Set your weight more toward your toes to help retain balance on the slope. Swing compactly and smoothly, and try to sweep the ball away—don't "dig" at it. The shot will tend to hook, so either allow for that or open the clubface at address to counteract it. Remember, too, that choking down on the shaft reduces distance, so take ample club.

BALL BELOW FEET.   Bend more than usually at the knees and grip the club at its very end, to bring your body as close as possible to its normal distance from the ball. To preserve your balance, set your weight more on your heels. Swing slowly and compactly, and keep your head still—any head movement or body sway on this shot can easily result in a shank. Try to retain your knee flex well into the follow-through. The ball will tend to fade, so either allow for that or close the clubface slightly at address.

ROUGH STUFF

People often comment that I play well from rough because I'm physically strong. The truth of the matter is that my ability—on occasion—to move the ball from hay has more to do with my style of swing than with muscular strength.

Obviously, the prime objective in playing from rough is to minimize the club's contact with it. Equally obviously, an upright swing achieves that objective better than a flat swing, because of the sharper angle at which the clubhead rises from and returns to the ball. Keep that in mind every time you enter the tall grass.

ESCAPE METHOD "A."   If distance is your objective from rough, play a "punch" shot. Move the ball back a little in your stance, close the clubface slightly, swing the club back on a very steep arc, and smash the clubhead sharply down into the back of the ball. Keep your legs and hips ahead of your hands through impact and hit hard with your right hand. The ball will come out low and fast and usually run a great distance, and you should allow for that long run.

ESCAPE METHOD "B." If height and stopping power are your objectives from rough, play a lob-type shot. Move the ball a little forward at address, aim a little left, open the clubface slightly, then swing in a normal arc but with plenty of wrist release through the ball. Stay behind the shot. The grass that intervenes between the clubface and the ball will reduce backspin, but the increased height from which the ball descends should help to soften its landing.

WOODS FROM ROUGH. The deeper down in the grass the ball lies, the less effective long irons become. Your fairway woods, with their smooth, rounded soles, give you a much better chance of sliding the clubhead through the grass without its slowing down or twisting off line. Technique? Stand a little more upright than usual. Position yourself with the ball back a couple of inches, open the clubface at address, swing back normally, and then pull sharply downward with the left arm and hit hard with the right hand. Allow for the ball to fade. This is a crude sort of shot—almost a "punch" shot—but you'll be surprised how much distance you get from what might have seemed at first glance a hopeless situation.

GRASS AGAINST SHOT. When the grass is growing away from the target it will tend to grab the clubhead and close the face, and it will also reduce distance by slowing down the clubhead. So take at least one more club than normal, grip firmly, aim to the right, and try to sweep the clubhead well down and under the ball so that it will rise quickly and thus avoid much of the grass.

GRASS WITH SHOT. Grass growing toward the target offers less resistance to the clubhead, but is almost certain to produce a "flyer." Therefore, take less club than you'd normally require, play for more height, and allow for more roll.

CHAPTER 10

Conditioning— or Confessions of a Long-Time Jock

I suppose I've always been an all-around jock of sorts. I like watching sports and talking sports, but most of all I like *doing* sports. I enjoy outdoor life and I enjoy physical exertion, but most of all I enjoy the challenges inherent in sports. I love to compete at just about anything, so long as I can do it half decently.

Thus I've always led a fairly athletic life, and I have to believe this has been beneficial to my golf. For example, all through this book I've stressed the importance of the legs in the golf swing. Even though my legs are naturally strong, they wouldn't do the job I call on them to do in a normal tournament day—practice before the round, four to five hours of walking, standing and playing, more practice after the round—if they weren't in good condition.

I think in the past three or four years there's been a sort of awakening in America to the fact that people just don't get enough exercise through the routine of their daily lives. This shows up with a vengeance in pro-ams, where we are normally playing with professional men and business executives. They sit in offices and cars all week, then ride around the course in golf carts all weekend. I'm often tempted to tell a fellow who's beating at the ball with his hands, or whaling around at it with his shoulders, to get more leg action into his swing. But how can the poor guy use something he hasn't got? Discouraging as it may sound, I must tell you that as long as your legs are in lousy shape you're never going to come anywhere close to reaching your full golfing potential.

I've never been a health fiend in the sense of muscle-building or fanatical dieting. But the benefits I derived from losing about 20 pounds in the fall of

1969 taught me a few things about how to live. For one thing, shedding that poundage increased my resistance to fatigue, and it also helped me to move faster through the ball. But the most important thing it did was to make me *feel* better, physically and about myself mentally. Thus, today, although I don't diet, I try to eat sensibly. I may have spaghetti and dessert for lunch one day, but the next I might eat shrimp and salad, or nothing at all. At times I have smoked off the golf course, but never to excess. And I drink a Scotch and water once in a while, or a little wine. But basically I just try to be normal: to stay in shape without carrying any crosses or getting too faddish about things.

Another thing the weight loss taught me was that the better the shape I stay in, the longer I'll go on playing golf decently. You don't see too many overweight fellows or heavy drinkers among the top senior golfers—and you certainly don't see the best of those seniors riding around in golf carts very often! I'm convinced that, as I get older, I shall increase, rather than decrease, the amount of exercising I do.

Apart from golf, I suppose tennis is my main form of exercise today. I used to game-fish a lot off the Florida and Bahamas coasts, and I still do on occasion, but that's not really exercise. I play baseball and football with my eldest sons and their pals. I swim and snorkel a bit with the kids, and I water-ski some. When my tournament days are over, I'll probably take up skiing—it's something I've always wanted to do. But over the past three or four years I've gotten pretty hooked on tennis. I started off playing at the Lost Tree Club near my home, but early in 1972 I built a court right in my backyard—it's one of the few grass courts in Florida. (Incidentally, some rather exaggerated stories seem to have spread around about my ability at tennis. I've heard people say that in

ANOTHER MUSCLE LOOSENER

Another good way to loosen golfing muscles is to swing two clubs at once. Hold a couple of irons with a baseball grip and swing them easily back and forth a few times. Don't try to swing fast. Just let the weight of the clubs gently loosen up your back, shoulder, leg, and arm muscles. You'll be surprised how light one club feels after this exercise. A weighted wood-head cover —most pros sell them—serves the purpose just as well as do a couple of clubs.

Hitting out a few balls with every second club in the bag is the finest way to warm up for a round of golf. Short of that, try the three simple muscle-looseners I always go through on the first tee (see text, page 195).

golfing terms I'm about a three-handicap player at tennis. Well, the truth is that, by my own standards, I'm about a twelve handicapper. But, because I really do hate doing anything badly, I intend to be a three before a couple more winters pass.)

Golf is my love and golf is my life, but candidly tennis seems to me in many ways a better game than golf. It's less expensive, takes less time, provides more exercise, demands as high a level of skill in a different way, is intensively competitive, can be played "mixed," and has fewer social or financial barriers. Probably I shouldn't even be saying this, but it's the way I feel. And it's why I've encouraged my wife, Barbara, to take up tennis instead of golf, and why I'd certainly not mind if my children preferred to play tennis rather than golf for exercise. I'd hope they'd want to play both, of course.

For the past year or so, when I've not been playing golf tournaments or traveling, I suppose I've played tennis just about every other day. I'll play either early in the morning, before going to my offices, or late in the afternoon after office hours. Mostly I play singles, and there's nothing I enjoy more than three sets against a better—but not too much better!—opponent. There's no finer workout in the whole world of sports.

Usually I cut down heavily on the tennis schedule about a week before an important tournament. I'm always a little concerned about the effect on my golf game of overexercising my right hand and arm. Even more important than this, though, is the effect of tennis on my legs. As great a leg conditioner as the game is, it takes three or four days for my legs to "relax" after a lot of tennis, for the muscles to regain the suppleness I need for golf. But my legs will always "come back" faster for golf if I've been playing tennis during a layoff from tournaments than if I haven't.

Beyond the activities I've mentioned, I do a few light exercises upon rising in the morning and often before going to bed at night. I run in place, touch my toes, bend and stretch; just enough to keep me supple around the middle. I don't make exercising any big deal, and I certainly don't spend the hours working out that Gary Player does (though, actually, I sometimes wonder how Gary does all the exercising he sometimes claims he does and still has time left to play golf!).

If you've watched me on the practice tee or the first tee at a tournament, you might have noticed a little warmup routine I always go through prior to my opening shot. I'm not going to give any lectures here about the value of hitting shots before playing—better men than I have failed to persuade weekend golfers to do that—but I would like to recommend this little regimen of mine to you, if only as a safeguard against strained muscles.

First I take a few full swings with a loose, wristy, flowing motion. This helps put some "feel" into my hands, and also loosens my wrist and forearm muscles. Next, I hold a club behind my back with my arms extended. Then I rotate my body back and forth from above the hips. This loosens the muscles in my upper back and shoulders. Finally, I hook the club through my elbows so that it lies across the middle of my back, then again rotate from the hips up. This stretches and loosens the muscles of my lower back.

The whole routine takes only a few seconds and by now has become second nature to me. I think it's one of the reasons I've so rarely suffered from muscular tears or strains in the twenty years I've been playing tournament golf of one sort or another.

CHAPTER 11

Practice:
How Much I Do and How I Do It

During my early years in golf I probably practiced as much as anyone in history, but today my temperament is such that I can only practice effectively when I have something specific to prepare for. Just going out and hitting balls for the sake of hitting balls doesn't do anything for me any more. Even playing just for the sake of playing doesn't necessarily help, although I'm sure it doesn't hurt. I'd rather play tennis, or work at my business involvements, or just spend time with my family around the house.

It's for this reason that I do almost all of what you might call my game-building practice in the first three months of the year, and virtually all of my fine-tuning practice at actual tournament sites. Candidly, even then I probably don't spend as much time on "misery hill" as do many of my contemporaries. I just don't see the need, for a couple of reasons.

First, I've been playing some sort of tournament golf now for over twenty years with never a break of more than a few weeks. Thus I don't totally "lose" my game during a layoff—I don't have to come back and start over from scratch. At thirty-four years of age, with all that golf behind me, the basics of my swing have become constant. The areas that need work to get it in shape are primarily tempo, rhythm, and coordination, and in my case they never necessitate hitting out a thousand balls a day.

The second reason I practice less than many other tour players is that whenever I do go out with a bag of balls I have a very specific objective in mind and, once I've achieved it, I quit. All my life I've tried to hit practice shots with great care. I try to have a clear-cut purpose in mind on every swing. I always practice as I intend to play. And I learned long ago that there is a limit to the number of shots you can hit effectively before losing your concentration on your basic objectives. I have to believe that some of the guys who virtually live on the practice tee out on tour are there because they don't have anything better to do with their time. And I have to believe they often weaken their games by letting their practice become pointless through sheer monotony or fatigue. But every man to his own poison, I guess. And I *am* talking about myself at this stage of my career. If I were talking about you, and you are a weekend golfer who wants to improve, I'd say something quite different. More practice, even at the expense of the fun of actual play, will pay dividends.

At the time I began working on this book, the 1972 golfing year was largely over for me in that I had no further major ambitions to try to fulfill. Thus I was at home a lot—where I prefer to be most anytime—and I was playing hardly any golf at all. To me, this was a time for relaxation, for clearing my mind of bad swing habits, for getting completely away from the game. Just to keep my hand in I might hit a few balls once every five or six days, but no more—often not even that.

AT-HOME PRACTICE

There are many things you can do to improve your golf without even leaving home.

I often check my swing in front of a mirror and track down a hitch in it that way. In fact, "mirroring" one's setup is one of the best ways I know to discover the root cause of inferior shot-making.

Other forms of indoor practice include hitting into a net; swinging a weighted club (or any heavy object); squeezing a hand exerciser, or practicing your grip on an actual golf club while, say, watching TV; putting on the rug; chipping into a basket. The possibilities are endless if you are really eager to improve your game.

What gets me going again, usually sometime around New Year's Day, is the thought of the upcoming Masters in April. This is always my first real goal of each year, my first incentive to start doing something significant about my shot-making. And, because preparing myself in actual competition is as vital to me as tuning my swing in practice, I get quite excited about the early-year tournaments. Really, deep down, they are just part of my preparation for Augusta. But that's generally enough of a prod to get me "up" for them.

Thus, usually early in January I will begin to work on my game at home. After a couple of sessions to get the cobwebs out, the first thing I always do is go down to see Jack Grout, at La Gorce Country Club in Miami Beach, for a lesson. We begin at the beginning, with the grip and the setup, and go right through the fundamentals. Apart from reinstilling their importance in my mind, this often has the effect of ironing out some of the bad habits I may have slipped into the previous year. I highly recommend this kind of periodic checkup to all golfers, whatever their ability. Even a par shooter can't see himself swing; he doesn't really know if he's doing what he thinks he's doing or wants to do. And the most futile thing of all, especially at the start of the year, is to waste all that new burst of enthusiasm on practicing imperfections.

Once Jack has straightened me out and I have a clear picture of what I want to achieve, I will sharply step up my practice sessions at home. I rarely hit balls for more than an hour at a time, because after that I begin to lose concentration and sight of my original shot-making goals. But maybe I'll have two one-hour sessions a day, or an hour on full shots and an hour chipping or hitting from sand or putting. As the regimen increases, I'll break it up with a few holes of actual play, to see how things are coming along. Usually, however, I play no more than nine holes at a time, because I can get so much more done in an hour on the practice tee than in a couple of hours on the course. During this period, whether it's practice or play, I make a special effort to avoid hitting shots carelessly. I give every shot my best try. Thus each shot takes thought and time, and I probably hit fewer balls per session than would most other players.

Once I'm sure my fundamentals are right, what I work for is "feel." If I interpret correctly the large amount of time some tour players practice, I imagine they must be seeking some kind of mechanical perfection; they're trying to become golfing automatons. I don't happen to believe that this is possible. To me, once your mechanics are reasonably sound, "feel" becomes the critical factor, and it changes from day to day with one's mood and metabolism. Thus, as my early-year, game-building practice develops, what I'm basically chasing are the various "feels" of the shots I want to hit. Once I've achieved a certain feel—by hitting, say, 10 consecutive shots the way I want to—I usually quit,

Every year, going into a new season, I take a refresher lesson from my lifelong teacher, Jack Grout. We begin at the beginning, with grip and setup, and go right through the fundamentals. There isn't a golfer in the world who wouldn't benefit from a similar periodic checkup.

WARM UP WITH THE CLUBS YOU LIKE

Don't make the mistake of turning preround warmup practice into a full-scale swing rebuilding session that leaves you blistered, bewildered, and badly demoralized.

Always start by hitting a few shots with the easiest clubs in the bag, the short irons. Then, as you go up the scale, pick the clubs in which you have most confidence. If you like the four-iron better than a three-iron, hit a few warmups with the four-iron and let the three lay. The same is true with the woods: If you're happier with the three-wood than the driver, warm up with the three-wood.

This way you'll be less tempted to start rebuilding your swing and more likely to build your confidence.

even if I've only been out there half an hour. Bill Casper is perhaps the closest tournament player to me in this respect. He goes out to practice with a specific purpose in mind and stops when he's achieved it. He doesn't believe in wasting energy and, more important, he knows the immense psychological value of ending on a positive note.

Sometimes, of course, the "feels" and the shots won't come. When that happens, I resist the temptation to fire balls off like a machine gun in a desperate hit-or-miss attempt to find the "secret." What I usually do is pack up the sticks, go home, sit down, and think about why I couldn't do what I wanted to do. I think in terms of cause and effect. I reflect on my bad shots and determine their cause. By next day I have what I hope is a logical picture in mind and a specific goal to achieve. If I fail again, I simply repeat the thinking-first, hitting-second process until I discover the true problem and the correct cure. Then I try to store this information away for future reference.

I am careful to practice under ideal conditions at the best locations. For example, I look for a piece of ground that gives me a perfectly level stance, especially when using the driver. I like to hit irons from firm, dry, close-cut turf. I prefer to practice all shots into a headwind because it magnifies any curving of the ball and thus demands maximum concentration and control on my part. Next best I prefer a right-to-left wind, but I avoid strong crosswinds because they do not tell me what I want to know about what I'm doing to the ball. I always use good, clean golf balls. And I always shoot to a specific target, like the caddie, or the shag bag, or a tree in the distance.

Of all the practice I do at home I'd guess 90 percent is devoted to full shots, the other 10 percent being spread between chipping, sand play, and putting. Starting in late February or early March I practice putting for about half an hour just about every day. As an admittedly inferior pitcher and chipper compared to the rest of my strokes, why don't I give more time to these departments of the game? The reason, I tell myself, is that my long game would deteriorate if I gave more time to the short game. Probably the truth is that I find practicing the short game comparatively boring.

Hopefully my game will be in reasonable shape by the time I get to my first tournament of the year, usually the Crosby. But I never expect too much of myself in the early events, because I know I need the stimulus of competition to sharpen my shot-making. I have to "play myself into shape" in tour competition. I simply can't do it knocking around the Florida golf courses with nothing but a few dollars in bets riding on the outcome.

Once the season is under way I do almost all my practicing at the tournament sites. The routine seldom varies. Mondays, if I'm not traveling, I normally take off completely; no shots, no play, just rest, or perhaps business, or whatever the family wants to do if they are out on tour with me. If there's any way I can spend Mondays at home—as I can, for example, when the tour's in Florida—I always do so. Tuesdays I will practice, play eighteen holes, then practice again. It's the same on Wednesday, except that I usually play my eighteen holes in the pro-am.

If I'm at home the week before a tournament, normally I'll go out only once and hit a few balls before the weekend. Then I'll practice maybe an hour on Saturday and perhaps another hour or two on Sunday. Monday I'll often play nine holes on the course then practice a little more. Monday night or Tuesday morning I'll head off to the tournament and pick up the regular tournament routine.

On tournament days I always practice before the round: full shots and putting, and sometimes a few chips and sand shots. Unless I am prevented from doing so—and the reason has to be a good one—I also practice after the round. Obviously the preround session is preparatory: warming up, getting the right "feels" going, determining the state of the union. But the postround session is equally important to me, in terms of relieving the day's tensions, correcting mistakes while they're still fresh in my mind, and preparing for the next day by rebuilding my confidence. I really hate to have to forego this end-of-day session.

I can often imagine the fan watching me practice at a tournament saying to himself: "Who is this guy Nicklaus, anyway? What's so good about him?" Because I can look absolutely terrible out there, even when I might be leading the tournament. One shot will fly low and hook, another low and fade. The next three might fly high and fade, the next two high and draw. Then perhaps I'll hit a straight shot, and then another low fade. While to a lot of people I must sometimes look like a real neophyte out there on the practice tee, the truth is, of course, that I'm hitting these different types of shots deliberately—at least most of them, anyway! I'm developing "feels," assessing my metabolism, and measuring my capabilities for the day.

The same thing is sometimes true even on the practice putting green. I'll be hitting the ball miles past or short of the hole, and I'll hear murmurings back there among the fans. One might whisper, "Heck, I can putt better than that guy!" Well, maybe he could, but he'd probably find me a little more consistent when we got out on the course. Because, again, what I'm doing is developing "feel": testing strokes, experimenting with different types of impact, trying to find the best peg for the day's greens work ahead.

By the time we approach the Masters each year I hope that the regimen I've described here will have brought my game to peak condition. If it has I don't need a lot more practicing in the physical sense, just the normal day-to-day fine tuning. Much more important then will be my mental state: how the year has been going for me generally; what's on my mind businesswise; whether I'm spending enough time with the children—the usual concerns and preoccupations of everyday living.

If the regimen hasn't worked, then major surgery may be necessary. I may have developed a particular flaw that I can't eradicate through my regular tourament-site practice schedule. In that case I'll usually take a week or more off from the tour, go home, do some hard thinking, and then go to work on my swing on a daily basis. But even then I have to be careful not to let any kind of overindulgence or desperation creep in. The mind always has to operate before the muscles go to work, and the muscles must only operate once the mind is working.

An example of how important it is to me to be able to analyze my faults mentally before I go to work on them physically is the trouble I've gone to to be able to record golf telecasts in which I'm involved. About two years ago, when video machines that would record from a home TV set first became available, I decided to buy one and to try to use it to study my own tournament play. Early in 1972 we installed the recorder in my den. Since then I've recorded, with the help of an old friend of mine, Sockeye Davis, just about every televised tournament in which I've been "on screen." An example of how this has helped my game was the U. S. Open at Pebble Beach in June of 1972. I was lucky enough to win it, but all during the championship I was bothered by two aspects of my play. First, I just couldn't seem to take the putter back smoothly, with the result that I found myself concentrating too much on the actual stroke and too little on sinking putts. The other problem was a sense of discomfort in my stance over the ball on full shots. After winning at Pebble Beach, I flew all night back home, and the first thing I did, even before sleeping, was to look at the 4½ hours of televised play. As soon as I watched my stance (crouched too much) and my putting stroke (I had dropped my right shoulder, making it awkward to take the putter back smoothly) I spotted my problems and was able to clear up both of them in a short practice session the next day.

I've described my personal practice and preparation program in some detail here strictly for whatever interest it might have for some readers. I am very well aware that much of it shouldn't apply for the average golfer, who plays maybe twice on weekends and occasionally during the week in the summer. He doesn't have the opportunity to work on his game as I do. I'm also aware that when such a fellow does get time for golf he wants to *play,* not beat practice balls into the blue yonder.

PLAY SOME "OPPOSITE" SHOTS IN EVERY SESSION

You'll maintain your interest in practicing, learn more about golf, and become a better player if you put some variety into your practice.

I frequently hit "opposite" shots when I'm practicing, to reduce the possibility of exaggerating any one particular aspect of my swing. For example, in a session where I'm basically trying to fade the ball, I'll intentionally hit two or three draws out of every twenty shots. It's challenging to "work" the ball, and it's also highly instructive to learn just what causes what results.

If you feel this is beyond you, at least try some half- and three-quarter shots with the various clubs you use. This is a great way to develop an advanced degree of tempo, rhythm, and control.

Well, that's just fine. If I were a weekend golfer I'd probably feel the same way. But the facts of the matter are inescapable. Nobody—but *nobody*—has ever become really proficient at golf without practice, without doing a lot of thinking and then hitting a lot of shots. It isn't so much a lack of talent; it's a lack of being able to repeat good shots consistently that frustrates most players. And the only answer to that is practice.

Your own experience probably proves this point. Every once in a while, even when you're not playing much, you'll hit a perfect shot, a shot as good as I or any other professional could hit. The more frequently you play—as, for example, when you're on vacation—the more you hit good shots; the less the incidence of really disastrous holes; over-all you become a better player. Right? *Right*. Now, you may tell yourself you're improving because you're *playing* more. But that really is not true. What you're really doing is *practicing* more. You just happen to be doing it on the course.

And you want to get better yet at golf? Well, the answer has to be plain: Just accelerate your rate of practice by going to the driving range a little more and to the course a little less.

PART THREE

Around and
On the Green

CHAPTER 1

Wedge Play and Other Pitches

I am at times only a fair short-iron player and a pretty ordinary wedge player. Admittedly, I set my standards high. To me, a perfect round of golf would be when one determines the perfect shot for each situation, then plays it perfectly. The closest I've ever come to that is maybe 75 percent, and generally I get no closer than 60 percent. And my highest rate of failure is most often on the shots from 125 yards in, because they require the highest degree of precision.

A few years back some of my friends on tour used to kid me that I was the only golfer in the world who was better with a one-iron than a nine-iron. At that time they weren't far from the mark. There has been some short-game improvement since then. I've learned a greater variety of short approach shots and improved my technique at many of them. Thus I feel I am slowly becoming more consistent and more confident with the pitching clubs. But there is still room for considerable improvement.

One reason why I'm a Little Leaguer at pitching as compared to a major leaguer like Deane Beman is simply because I haven't had to play as many wedge shots as he has. Normally I can reach the greens on long par-4 holes—even some par-5s—in 2 shots, where Deane might need 3. Thus, only when I've played courses with lots of drive-and-pitch par-4s (rare in championship golf), or when I've been playing very badly, have I had much pitching practice in actual play.

Another reason for my inferior pitching is the fact that the courses I grew up on in Ohio didn't have the type of turf that called for a lot of spinning of the

BE DECISIVE ON "PART" SHOTS

I believe the main reason some weekend players can't play anything but full shots with the wedge is because they never clearly make up their minds how much "power" they should use. You must decide on any "part" shot whether you will swing firmly or easily. If you don't, indecision in midswing will certainly wreck the shot. I prefer a relatively firm approach any time I can, and I think it's best for most golfers because it requires less swing finesse than does "softing" the ball. The trick, either way, is to fit the length of the backswing to the distance of the shot— make it just long enough to produce good rhythm and avoid jabbing, but not so long that you will decelerate or "quit" on your downswing. "Measure" or "feel" the amount of backswing you need with a few thoughtful practice swings.

ball with the short irons. You could usually stop the ball on the green with a kind of soft lob shot; a semi-"flier" really. Thus I could often get away with less than 100 percent striking perfection on the shorter approach shots, and this, in my case, obviously bred a little carelessness or laziness. When I first went on tour the variety of turf and lies I encountered often foxed me completely. It was really only after I came to live in Florida that my wedge play began to improve, as a result of practicing and playing from Bermuda grass, from which the ball must be struck very accurately and authoritatively to get good results.

Variety is the name of the pitching game. The greater the variety of shots you can play around the green, the better you'll score. The British writers call this the art of "manufacturing" shots, and the word perfectly describes what is involved. Although each shot is played within the framework of the basic swing, subtle changes in technique are needed to produce particular flight and roll effects. In both pitching and chipping the list of such finesse shots is endless, and I don't suppose any golfer ever learns them all. But the more you can master, the more often you'll turn three shots into two, thus the better you'll score, especially when you're playing poorly from tee to green—as exemplified by Bobby Locke, Billy Casper, Gary Player, and many other top golfers.

Within this chapter I will describe a few of the pitching variations I em-

"PUNCHING" WEDGES

You can "punch" the ball lower than normal with the more lofted clubs, but you'd probably achieve the same effect more easily by playing a half shot with a less lofted club. If you do decide to "punch" with the wedges, move the ball back a little, swing firmly, and hit hard with your hands through impact. But keep your hands ahead of the ball, and the right hand "under" the left hand well through impact.

ploy from day to day, but as all these "special" shots are really derivations of my two basic types of pitch shot it would be as well first to look more closely at those. I should point out here that I play all the shots described in this chapter primarily with the pitching wedge and the sand wedge or, occasionally, with the eight- or nine-iron.

Perhaps I should also mention again that basic swing fundamentals don't change. My arc and plane are governed by the length of the club and the way I set up to each shot. I stand a little "open" to most pitch shots, just as I do to

A TIME FOR THE SAND WEDGE

Most amateurs seem to think that the sand wedge is the last club to consider using to pitch from a hard, bare, or sandy lie. To me it's the first. By aiming fractionally behind the ball—not more than half an inch—you give yourself a margin for error with this deeply flanged club that doesn't exist with the sharper-edged pitching wedge. If you catch the ball just right with either club, well and good. But if you hit a little behind it with a sand wedge, its deep flange often allows the club to bounce or skid along and graze under the ball. A pitching wedge or nine-iron, on the other hand, would simply dig straight into the ground.

"SWEEPING" FROM SPONGY TURF

Even if the lie is good, on a short shot from just off the green I often "sweep" the ball with a wedge rather than chip it with a less lofted club. This way—especially from soft or spongy turf—I find I can make more solid contact, and thus maintain better control, than by hitting down on the ball, as in a chip shot. Properly played this way the ball flies fairly high and lands very softly. The danger, of course, lies in scooping under, rather than sweeping through, the ball. Practice is essential.

most full shots. My body action is only a miniature version of my full-shot action; the lesser amount of power being applied, the shorter my turn and swing arc. I try to swing the club straight through low along the target line and on out toward the target without rolling my hands and wrists, unless I'm seeking some special spin effect. And I try to maintain the same slow tempo and smooth rhythm I use for the longer shots with the longer clubs.

When the pin is positioned so that there is room for the ball to take one good-sized bounce before it stops, I will generally try to backspin a firm, relatively low-flying pitch shot into the green. To achieve this effect, I play the ball about an inch farther back in my stance, thereby positioning my hands a little farther ahead of it than normal. This change in "geometry" establishes a steeper

"BLASTING" FROM GRASS

Stopping the ball quickly from greenside rough is never an easy shot, but I often play it just as I do a blast from sand: Clubface open at address, abrupt or steep backswing arc, contact about an inch behind the ball while keeping my right hand well "under" my left. Properly played, the ball will rise quickly and drop softly. But again, don't try it without practice.

Many a golfer misses less-than-full shots because he does not match the length of his backswing to the distance the ball must travel. Sometimes an overabbreviated backswing leads to a hurried, jerky downswing in a last-second effort to generate the missing power. More commonly, the golfer overswings going back, then decelerates coming down so as not to hit the shot into the next county. The solution is to "measure" the size of backswing required with a few practice swings, then smoothly accelerate the club from that point through the ball.

MAXIMUM SPEED

MAXIMUM SPEED

MORE WRISTS FOR EXTRA HEIGHT AND BACKSPIN

If I want a lot of height on a fullish pitch shot, I break or cock my wrists quickly on the backswing, then use them very actively to "throw" the club under—not down on—the ball. Properly executed, this flips the ball high with good backspin.

swing arc, which promotes a sharper, crisper, more acutely downward delivery of the club to the ball. This in turn produces more backspin.

At address for this type of shot, I normally square the clubface to the target. Playing the ball back sets my weight predominantly on my left side, and I keep it there throughout the shot. This helps promote the steep swing arc that also adds backspin. Any time I move the ball back in my stance there's a real danger I'll hit it too much from the inside—when the clubhead is still looking to the right and moving in that direction. To obviate this tendency I try to swing slightly across the ball from out to in—to put a little cut on it. Otherwise I swing normally, but always very firmly, subconsciously adjusting the length of the swing to the distance of the shot.

I'll use this type of shot whenever I can from about 125 yards in, because there is relatively little chance of hitting it fat—digging in behind the ball. It's a good shot from close lies, but it does require a generous green area and a holding surface. It's an especially fine shot in wind, but it requires a firm stroke

GRASSY LIES

The prime objective on any shot from a grassy lie is to minimize the amount of grass that gets between ball and club-face at impact. To reduce this interference, I move the ball back an inch or so in my stance, open the clubface, aim left to allow for a fair amount of fade, swing steeply, and think of making a full follow-through to be sure I swing smoothly *through* the ball.

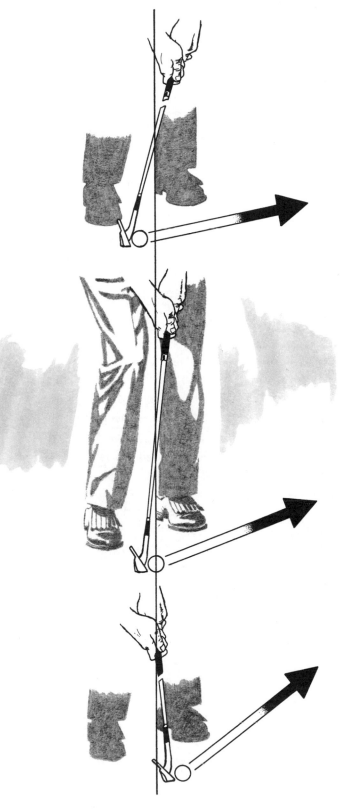

By decreasing effective clubface loft, moving the hands closer to the target at address produces lower-flying pitch and chip shots. Conversely, moving the hands away from the target at address produces higher-flying shots by increasing the club's effective loft. Another way to vary height is to position the hands normally and simply play the ball farther back or forward in relation to the feet.

played confidently: Faintheartedness spells disaster in the form of either a flub or a skull. Thus, if you fancy adding this shot to your own armory, I suggest you practice it a lot first.

If the greens are firm or the pin position necessitates stopping the ball "dead" without much bounce, or if there is a high obstacle between the ball and my target, or if any of these factors combine, I normally try to throw in a gentler, higher-flying, softer-landing kind of shot. Here some backspin is obviously required, but I depend mostly on the ball "floating" almost vertically downward to its target to minimize roll.

To achieve this result I basically just reverse the former setup procedure, then make a softer swing. I position the ball an inch farther forward than

PITCHING FROM DOWNHILL AND UPHILL LIES

The toughest thing to do on a downhill pitch shot—just as on a downhill full shot—is to contact the ball before the club catches the hillside behind it. I often try to achieve this solid contact simply by staying well ahead of the ball—my weight on my left side—and then emphasizing right-hand action to throw the clubface under the ball. Extending through the ball in a down-the-slope swing path is essential to prevent topping. Remember, too, that the slope will tilt you to the left and thus reduce the club's effective loft and thereby the height of the shot.

An uphill lie, when it's a good one, presents a relatively easy shot, so long as you *sweep* rather than *punch* the ball by making the swing arc follow the ground contour. Remember that the slope will increase the effective loft of the club; thus the ball will fly higher and shorter than normal. If the ball's on an uphill lie but buried in rough, as often happens on a grassy bank beside a green, there's little choice but to chop directly into the ball, as though the lie were flat. Play for the ball to pull a bit to the left of target, a result of the fact that the hill will prevent you from using full leg action on your forward swing. Open the clubface, hit firmly, and keep your head still and your eyes on the ball.

THE PITCH AND RUN

Heavy watering has removed the necessity for the pitch-and-run shot on many U.S. courses, but if you play in Britain, or on dry and windy courses in the States, you'd better have it in your repertoire. Often in the British Open—and sometimes in the U.S. Open, too—conditions are such that it is the best percentage shot. I will pitch and run the ball with just about any club from a five-iron down, but I prefer the seven- and eight-irons. I always try to land the ball short of the green on the flattest available piece of ground, to avoid trick bounces. I play the ball back an inch or so in my stance, choke down on the club, make a firm, upright backswing, and concentrate on meeting the ball very solidly without collapsing my left wrist through impact. In picturing the shot beforehand I usually will see about half of the ball's journey as flight and the other half as roll.

normal with my hands in their usual position, which has the effect of bringing them almost even with the ball. Mostly I open the clubface a little at address, and achieve a slight out-to-in swing pattern by setting up left of target. I distribute my weight at address evenly on both feet, and I make a conscious effort to stay behind the ball through impact. I swing normally but relatively slowly, with a distinct feeling of slinging the clubhead through the ball, much as you would toss a golf ball underhand to a fellow player on the green. Thus, on this shot, my downswing arc is less sharply descending. It's more level through impact so that the effective loft of the clubface is increased, imparting less "bite" to the ball. The clubhead throws the ball more up than forward.

Again, I'll use this shot to cover any distance up to about 125 yards. Ideally it is a shot to be played from a lush lie. It is not a good shot to play in high wind unless no other will do. It also requires practice in order to be played confidently, especially from a close lie.

Most of my short approach shots, of course, fall somewhere between these two extremes. But they are my basics—and they represent an area of my game that will soon be getting some further attention in my practice sessions.

CHAPTER 2

Chipping: A Multifaceted Art

For a long time I felt that my chipping was often on a par with my wedge play —somewhere between fair and lousy. I guess the same reasons applied; I just didn't play enough chips on the course or, perhaps more significantly, to the practice green. I've gotten better in the past two or three years, but there is still plenty of room for improvement.

I find it difficult to write about chipping in a way that will make much sense to anyone looking for technical help in this area of the game. For one thing, I don't really know where chipping starts and stops in the area between pitching and putting. To me, the techniques meld into each other. For another thing, there are so many different ways to chip—I think I could chip balls for an hour or more without ever repeating myself. Then, too, as in putting there are so many different mechanical ways of doing the job—so many obviously successful but technically diverse methods. Moreover, there is the most complex variable of all, the "touch" factor. It wasn't just good technique that made people like Bobby Locke, Jerry Barber, and Billy Casper great chippers; it was "touch," a particular kind of sensitivity, both in the mental reading and the physical execution of the shot. You might possess a fine natural touch, or you might be able to develop one through practice, but I can't teach it to you by the printed word, and neither can anyone else.

Obviously, the closer you get to the hole in golf, the more critical becomes

THE ONE-CLUB APPROACH

I understand that Bobby Locke, one of golf's all-time great chippers as well as putters, did all his chipping with a pitching wedge. Increasingly in recent years I have come to rely on the sand wedge for a great variety of shots around the green. One reason for this one-club approach is that I can become more expert and confident in an hour's practice with one club than I could by giving, let us say, six clubs ten minutes' work apiece.

I still use other clubs down to the five-iron for chipping, but I believe there'll come a day when I'll rely almost entirely on finessing the sand wedge and using just one other club—probably a six-iron—when I need an unusually long roll.

the picture you paint in your mind before you play the shot. Because of the many variables involved—speed, break, relative amounts of flight and roll—chipping demands particularly clear and accurate headwork. In my case, I employ much the same four-step mental process on chip shots as on full shots. First, I "read" the situation. Then I picture a shot to fit it. Then I match a club to the picture. Finally I match a technique to the club. Without this kind of careful preparation, getting the ball consistently close to the hole from around the green would be impossible for me. And even after all that, my "touch" during execution will be the make-or-break factor.

I play basically three kinds of chip shots, all of which are really just scaled-down versions of my basic pitch shots. One produces a fast-running or far-

PLAY FOR MAXIMUM ROLL

To me, roll is easier to judge than flight. Thus, generally, my policy in chipping is to land the ball from 4 to 5 feet into the green and let it roll the rest of the way—particularly on smooth, level greens.

LEAD CLUBFACE WITH HANDS

Scooping under the ball in an attempt to get it airborne is a frequent mistake high handicappers make, usually resulting in anything from actually digging into the turf behind the ball to a topped shot. You'll beat this tendency if you keep your head very still, your left shoulder "low," and make sure that your hands lead the clubface into and through the ball. Consciously hit a little down into the ball, but, most importantly, feel that you "pull" the clubface *through* the ball with your hands.

running ball: I think of it as a "hot" ball. The second produces a soft-landing or quick-stopping ball, and I think of this as a "dead" ball. The in-between shot produces a ball that rolls on landing about the same distance as it has traveled through the air, and I don't think of it as anything but a short pitch-and-run shot.

I give each of these shots its particular characteristic by manipulating the clubface through impact with my hands and wrists. Apart from these variations, which we'll come back to, my chipping setup and stroke are pretty unvarying.

I use a very narrow stance and a slightly open body-alignment. My weight

"FEEL OUT" EACH SHOT WITH YOUR PRACTICE SWING

Normally a practice swing before a full shot on the golf course is merely a tension reliever and muscle loosener, but on short shots, and particularly on chip shots, it serves as a "rehearsal" for the actual stroke. Make a few practice swings that duplicate the swing with which you intend to hit the ball. You'll notice that most pro tour players do this prior to playing all chip and pitch shots. They are simply "measuring" or feeling out the exact length and force and type of swing needed to execute the shot correctly.

TOO HARD OR TOO SOFT?

If your chips fly too low and run too far, there's a good possibility that you are rolling your wrists in a counterclockwise
direction through impact. If your chips fly too high and stop too
quickly, check for the opposite hand-wrist motion. If your hands
work too much "under," or clockwise, through impact, you'll
open the clubface and thus "soften" the shot.

is predominantly on my left side and remains there throughout the shot. I position the ball opposite my left heel, but because my feet are so close together the
ball is, in effect, almost centered between my feet. It is also close in to my feet,
for a couple of reasons: first, to enable me to position my eyes directly over it
and the target line; second, to promote a straight-back, straight-through clubhead path. Normally I choke well down on the club—to within an inch or two
of the steel—to increase my control. Normally, too, because my left arm and
the club form a straight line to the ball from my left shoulder, my hands are
slightly ahead of the ball at address. My concept of the ideal chipping stroke is
that it should be firm but easy, and slow but accelerating at impact. Thus,
whatever type of chip shot I'm playing, I strive for a deliberate but a "quiet"
tempo.

My grip depends on the type of chip I am playing. Usually with the

PUSHED AND PULLED CHIPS

Pushing chips off to the right or pulling them left is often
the result of playing the ball too far from your body. This encourages you to swing the club with your shoulders rather than
your hands, wrists, and forearms. Just move up close enough so
that you don't have to turn your shoulders to swing the club. If
that doesn't do the job, check your ball positioning. Pushing can
result from playing the ball too far back, and pulling from positioning it too far forward.

CHIPPING FROM SAND

Chipping from sand traps, given a good lie and a low front lip, is not as difficult as many weekend golfers imagine. Take an eight- or nine-iron, play the ball back in your stance, choke up on the grip, then hit firmly down on the upper back part of the ball. Keep your head *particularly* still on this shot: The slightest head movement, especially of the up-and-down variety, will produce disaster.

wedges, or when I'm playing, in effect, a semi-pitch or a pitch-and-run shot, I employ my normal full-shot interlocking grip. As the stroking action gets closer to my putting stroke, I usually switch to the reverse-overlap grip that I use for putting, especially in playing little running chips from the fringe (see chapter "Putting: That Other Game"). In either case, I hold the club firmly but not tightly.

I am essentially a wrist chipper. I strive for a minimum of body movement, and just enough arm swing going back to promote a free hinging of the wrists (obviously, the longer the shot the more the arms must swing). On very short chips, the sort that are really no more than lofted putts, there is hardly any arm movement at all on my backswing, but rather just a slight backward wrist break. However, on the through swing on all chip shots my arms must obviously swing forward if I am to "lead" or "pull" the clubhead cleanly through the ball with my hands and wrists.

The infinite variety of course and weather conditions encountered by the tournament golfer demands that he learn to "finesse" the ball, especially around the greens. Thus I've gradually developed quite a variety of chipping techniques, two of them illustrated here. By swinging the clubface through the ball from open to closed (top drawing), I'm able to produce a low-flying, far-running kind of shot—a "hot" ball, I call it. Reversing the process, I produce a higher-flying, softer-landing chip shot—I think of it as a "dead" ball—by swinging the clubface through the ball from closed to open. Neither technique is beyond the reasonably skillful golfer who'll give some time to practicing these finesse shots.

RUNNING CHIP

STOPPING CHIP

CHIPPING PRACTICE

To improve your touch or technique during practice sessions, don't chip one shot and then change clubs and locations to chip another. Take one club and work on it from one spot until you can consistently repeat the shot you're trying to play. Only then move on to another club and another location.

For the "hot" ball that runs forward, I turn the clubface in an open-to-closed pattern through the ball. Going back, my hands rotate clockwise a little as my wrists hinge so that the back of my left hand eventually faces more outward than down. I return the club to the ball predominantly with my right hand, allowing it to roll over the left hand through impact. The resulting closing action of the clubface keeps the ball low and imparts a little hook spin to it: thus the "hot," running ball.

Playing the "dead" ball, I simply reverse the "hot" ball pattern by swinging the club very slightly from closed to open. Going back, my hands rotate counterclockwise slightly as my wrists hinge so that the back of the left hand eventually faces more down than forward. Returning the club to the ball, I control it predominantly with my left hand, thus insuring that my right hand works "under" rather than "over" the left through impact. The resulting opening action of the clubface gives height to the shot and imparts a little cut spin to it: thus the "dead" landing. I will, incidentally, often use this technique on a long, low-flying chip where I want the ball to stop fairly quickly.

On the in-between shots, the sort of small pitch-and-run shot where I want both flight and roll, I simply eliminate the hand manipulation. No wrist rolling —I swing the clubface back squarely and through squarely in a joint effort with both hands.

My "hot" shot and my "dead" shot are really just scaled-down versions of my draw and fade on full shots. As in my long game, they come in many shades, and I'll play them with all kinds of clubs and with varying mental swing pictures, depending on the situation and my mood or metabolism.

CHAPTER 3

Sand:
Skimming Is the Trick

The best sand player I have ever seen is, without doubt, Gary Player. He's miraculous from just about all types of sand and from every kind of lie. Playing against him, you begin hoping he'll be on grass rather than in sand anytime he misses a green. From grass you expect him to pitch or chip the ball close to the hole. From a bunker you're afraid he'll hole it out!

Despite occasional lapses—like twice taking 2 shots to get out of traps at Merion in the 1971 U. S. Open playoff against Lee Trevino—I think of myself as being a satisfactory bunker player. Not in the Player class, of course. But steady. I can get up and down in 2 shots, say, three out of five times.

If today I am at least competent from sand, once again the man I have to thank is Jack Grout. Early in 1967 I'd lost a certain amount of confidence in bunkers, especially in very soft or powdery sand and in synthetic sand or silica (which I still hate because of its lack of resistance to the club). I was failing to get the ball up high enough or far enough on too many simple bunker shots around the green. I knew the reason: I was digging the club too deeply into the sand. But I couldn't figure out *why* I was doing so.

Consequently, after the second round of the Florida Citrus Open, in Orlando, I decided once again to seek the help of my ever-reliable teacher. That evening I flew down to Miami and Jack was kind enough to go straight out onto the course with me at La Gorce. I hit a few sand shots, and it was apparent

223

SLOW-MOTION TEMPO WORKS BEST IN SAND

Anxiety about getting out of sand—and sometimes even embarrassment about having gotten into it—causes many golfers to rush their swings on bunker shots. This is a bad mistake and usually a costly one. The number of factors that must be taken into account on a sand shot demands calm and careful study of each situation, and then a slow-tempo swing that allows maximum club control. This is so important to me that I often think of swinging literally in slow motion when I'm in sand.

that I was still doing basically what he'd taught me as a kid in Ohio: stance open; clubface open; ball opposite left toe; full upright swing; right hand moving "under" left hand through impact to keep the clubface open; meeting the sand an inch or two behind the ball; full follow-through; slow, easy tempo.

Jack didn't really change any of this, but by then he'd developed some new ideas on bunker play, a kind of evolution from the basically orthodox method he'd taught me in Columbus. The key to height and distance, he'd now come to believe, was not how far behind the ball the club enters the sand per se, but how *deeply* under the ball the clubhead travels—in other words, how much sand you take.

Thus, the first new concept he put in my mind that evening was one of *removing a section of sand,* rather than of hitting to a point in the sand. You'll get the idea if you picture the ball on the sand in the center of, say, a 6-inch-long-by-3-inch-wide rectangle. You're now going to remove not the ball but the rectangle of sand beneath it, to a depth of, say, half an inch. And you're going to do this on every shot where the ball is lying cleanly, varying the height and distance of each shot by the amount you open the clubface and the length or force of your swing. For a very short, high, dead-landing shot you open the clubface very wide and swing very softly. For a little longer shot, you open the clubface a little less and swing a little more fully and firmly. And so on. But on every shot you remove from beneath the ball the same rectangle of sand, to the same depth.

To help me master this concept Grout suggested a slight change in my

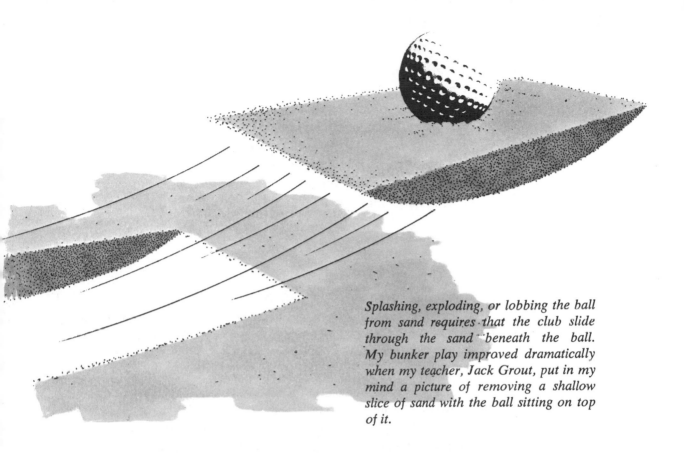

Splashing, exploding, or lobbing the ball from sand requires that the club slide through the sand beneath the ball. My bunker play improved dramatically when my teacher, Jack Grout, put in my mind a picture of removing a shallow slice of sand with the ball sitting on top of it.

THE EASIEST AND THE TOUGHEST SAND

Many golfers fear wet sand. They shouldn't. It's the easiest type to play from, because it promotes clubhead "bounce" as opposed to "dig." The depth of the cut is the most difficult thing to control on sand shots, but less so in wet sand because the moisture increases its resistance to the club.

The less resistance the sand offers, the more the club will tend to dig, and the more it digs the faster it slows down. Thus the toughest traps are those filled with powdery or synthetic silica sand. Here, the depth of your cut must always be very finely judged and controlled to achieve the desired effect. That's why you'll generally see me in the practice bunker more often than usual at a tournament where the sand in the traps is powdery or synthetic.

setup and a slight change in the way I swung the club. At address he had me position my hands opposite the clubface, or even a little behind it. I could see how this would help to promote the necessary skimming, rather than a chopping, action of the clubhead through the ball. Then Jack asked me to "release" the clubhead earlier in the downswing, by putting my right hand more in control of it: He asked me, in effect, to hit more "from the top." This again, he maintained, would help to promote a skimming rather than a chopping action through impact by widening or "flattening" the bottom of the swing arc. As soon as Jack had suggested it, this earlier release of the club through right-hand action rang a bell in me. I'd always done that when feathering little wedge shots from good lies in grass. Why not do the same when I wanted a high, dead-landing ball from sand?

Grout suggested I consider making this my basic technique from sand around the green, and he also give me another piece of good advice about bunker play. He suggested that henceforth I vary the depth of the cut of sand I wanted to take, not by moving the ball about in my stance or changing my swing arc (the generally accepted methods) but simply by altering the relationship of my hands to the clubface at address. For the very shallow cuts, what I had to do was position my hands well behind the clubface at address. For a slightly deeper cut, I would move my hands forward to about opposite the ball. For an even deeper cut, I'd move them a little ahead of the ball. For a deeper cut still, I'd move them yet farther ahead of the ball. And so on. And in every case I could set up and then swing normally without any conscious swing-arc adjustments.

I took Jack's advice on all points, and my sand game showed a little more polish immediately. Then, shortly after that session, I made a further discovery of my own. In an effort to maintain a slow and easy tempo on sand shots I'd been letting my body "flow" into the shot too much; I'd developed a kind of tilting forward sag, or sway, on the forward swing and the through swing. "You don't do that on any other shot," I told myself. "You hit against a firm left side. Why not in sand?" As soon as I firmed up my left side I knew I had put the finishing touch to Jack's lesson. The forward sagging had obviously contributed to, if not caused, my "digging" tendency, by steepening my forward-swing arc. With my left side firmed up the problem vanished. And, with Jack's new concepts in the works, my bunker play began to improve immeasurably.

As with pitching and chipping, it would be possible to write a whole book on all the various types of shots one is called upon to play from sand: clean lies and buried lies, uphill and downhill lies, different textures of sand, short shots

(Left) Some tour professionals vary the depth at which they cut through the sand beneath the ball by changing the arc of the swing—steep for a deep cut, shallow for a light cut. I achieve the same effect, more simply and reliably I believe, merely by altering the relationship of my hands to the clubface at address and impact. Starting with my hands well behind the clubface for the shallowest of cuts, I simply move them progressively farther forward in relation to the clubface the deeper I want to slide the club beneath the ball.

(Below) Releasing earlier with the right hand—almost a "hitting-from-the-top" action—promotes skimming the sand with a shallow cut by "flattening" the bottom of the swing arc. In using this technique it is imperative to work the right hand "under" the left hand through impact.

In attempting to maintain a soft, flowing tempo on sand shots, it is easy to fall into the habit of sagging or swaying the body forward during the downswing. I improved my sand play immeasurably some years ago simply by firming up my left side. By keeping my body behind the ball through impact, I cured my tendency to dig the clubhead too deeply into the sand.

ALLOW FOR CUT SPIN

Most sand shots are played with an outside-to-inside club-head path. Thus there will usually be a tendency for the ball to hop from left to right upon landing. You should allow for this by aiming a bit left of target.

However, when you have to chop the ball from a buried lie there will usually be no sidespin and very little backspin, so here you must allow for a long, straight roll.

and long shots, fast-stopping and hard-running shots. I'm not going to elaborate on all of these, first because I think it would be very confusing to the reader, and second because I think you can only learn the finer points of sand play through experience and practice. Instead, I'll simply cover here a few of the generalities about bunker play that seem most important to me.

First, about the sand club itself. We'll take it for granted that you know why you can't play sand shots as well as you might if you use a club without a flange that angles down lower than its leading edge. But be careful about *how much* flange you select. To my mind a sand club with a very deep flange is dangerous on any shot where the lie of the ball is less than perfect. The reason is that the deeper the flange, the more the club will bounce along the surface of the sand rather than cut through it beneath the ball. Thus, on any shot that

A WAY TO GAUGE SWING FORCE

The abiilty to gauge how hard to swing in sand really comes only through experience and practice, but a rule of thumb that has served me well at times is to think of swinging twice as hard as I would for a pitch shot of the same distance. If I have a 15-yard sand shot, I'll swing about as hard as I would for a 30-yard pitch. If the sand shot is 30 yards, I'll think of and try to apply the swing force I would use on a 60-yard pitch shot.

GOLF MY WAY
Jack Nicklaus

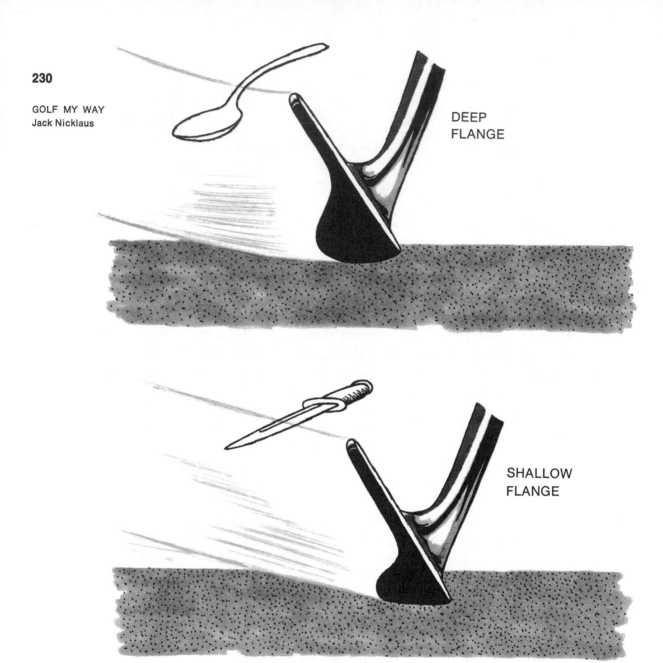

DEEP
FLANGE

SHALLOW
FLANGE

The deeper the flange, the more the sand wedge will bounce along the surface of the bunkers and the tougher it will be to slide the club beneath the ball, especially on less-than-perfect lies or in wet sand. On the other hand, a shallow-flange may knife too readily into the sand, especially the powdery or silica types. That's why I prefer a medium-flanged bunker club.

presents a less-than-perfect lie, you risk bouncing a very deep-flanged club into, rather than knifing it under, the ball. Result: a skulled shot. It's for this reason, and also because I like to use the sand wedge for pitching and chipping from grass, that I prefer only a medium-depth flange on my sand wedge.

The next point about sand play is to dig in with the feet, not the club. The less securely your feet are planted the worse your chance of keeping your balance during any golf shot. The way to get a firm footing in sand is to squirm your feet well down into it. And there's an excellent reason for doing this beyond that of producing stability. The rules of golf do not allow you to touch the sand with your hands or the club, but they do not prevent you from assessing its consistency with your feet. So use them to help determine what kind of shot you must play, as well as to give yourself the soundest possible swing base.

Another principle of sand play is that you contact the ball before the sand only when you need lots of distance. The more distance you want, the more cleanly you should try to contact the ball. Yet another principle is that the more height you want and the more backspin you want, the more the clubface must remain open through impact, and the thinner the slice it should take through the sand beneath the ball. Thus, for full height and backspin you must set up and swing in a way that promotes an open clubface and a shallow-bottomed swing arc. Yet another principle is that the more sand the clubface must cut through in order to work under the ball, the less open the clubface must be and the more sharply it must descend into the sand behind the ball. Thus the deeper you are buried the more you must set up and swing in a way that promotes a square to slightly closed clubface and a steep arc—a "knifing" action as the club enters the sand.

Once a golfer understands these basic technical principles I think he has only two further requirements to become at least capable of getting the ball on

A SHARPER EDGE HELPS ON BURIED LIES

The deeper the ball is buried, the tougher it becomes to get the club down and under it. In some situations a thinner-flanged, sharper-edged club than the sand wedge will do a better job of "knifing" down and under. Thus you should consider using the pitching wedge or nine-iron to remove a badly buried ball.

PUTTING FROM SAND

Putting from a greenside trap can sometimes be a good-percentage shot if the ball is sitting up on firm and level sand, and if there is relatively little frontal lip to the bunker. In playing such a shot I use my normal putting stroke with one exception: I hit the ball off the *toe* of the putter. Reason? This type of contact seems to reduce backspin (yes, even putts sometimes backspin) and promotes immediate forward rolling. But you must stroke the ball firmly to compensate for the power you'll lose from the off-center contact.

the green most of the time. The first is some practice in sand—and the only thing I'll say further on that score is that many of the amateurs I play with in pro-ams look as though they're going into sand for the first time in their lives when they step into a trap. The second essential is the adoption of a highly pragmatic attitude toward bunker play. Some things are possible from sand and some things are not, and you have to know the difference and accept it if you are to avoid catastrophes. For example, let's go back to our final principle: The deeper the ball is imbedded in sand, the more sharply you must dig the club down behind it to "knife" it out. Well, obviously the more you dig down, the more sand you take. The more sand you take, the less backspin you can impart to the ball. The less backspin the ball carries, the farther it will run. Thus, if you have a deeply buried ball but only a few feet of green to work with, you have an almost impossible shot in terms of getting the ball close to the hole. In situations like this—and there are many of them in bunker play—you simply have to modify your goal. You may have to accept just getting the ball safely somewhere on the putting surface, and then concentrating on making your best possible putt.

I know from experience how tough that sort of medicine is to take, but sometimes there's just no way out but to swallow it, even if afterward you cry a little to yourself.

CHAPTER 4

Putting:
That Other Game

BELIEFS AND ATTITUDES

I am often asked whether I think putting is too important in golf. The answer is that I do. But I believe the fault isn't so much in the basic nature of the game as in its modern evolution. What has given putting its present pre-eminence— on the U.S. professional tour, at least—are the improvements in equipment and playing techniques that have evolved in the past fifty years or so, plus the types of courses that have proliferated in America in recent years.

Golf's Scottish fathers certainly didn't intend the game to be the way it is today. In fact, if they'd had anything like today's clubs and balls and swing techniques, I'm certain they would have built 9000-yard courses—and maybe 6-inch holes. In the old days, getting to the green was what sorted out the men from the boys. Among today's tour players shadings in shot-making ability are very faint. Everybody gets to the green in pretty much the same number of strokes. Undoubtedly, the majority of present-day tournaments are decided on the putting surface.

I regard myself as a good putter, not a great putter like Arnold Palmer; in his heyday Arnie was the greatest putter I've ever seen. But if you take my career over-all, I've certainly not been a bad putter, despite some occasional pretty awful slumps. Furthermore, I enjoy putting as much as any other part of golf—when I'm not doing it on those big, soft, throw-a-driver-in-and-it'll-stick turf nurseries that some architects call greens. Therefore I have no personal ax to grind. But I do feel fairly strongly that, for a long time now, we've

"CHARGE" OR "DIE"

On the assumption that by knowing exactly what you are trying to do you give yourself the best chance of doing it, I think you should decide whether you are by nature or choice a "charge" or a "die" putter.

Arnold Palmer was, of course, the greatest "charge" putter in history. His policy was to hit the back of the hole hard enough and true enough to "trap" the ball into the cup.

I'm a "die" putter, in the sense that I aim to drop the ball just over the front lip of the cup when I stroke it perfectly, or, hopefully, let it topple in from the sides when I don't. One reason I prefer this technique to Arnold's is that it's less wearing on the nerves, especially as one grows older and those 3-foot comeback putts start looking like 15-footers. But if you putt this way, you should have the old maxim in your mind, "Never up, never in." Putt to let the ball "die" at the hole—not before it ever gets there!

been going architecturally in some wrong directions in American golf, and that this mis-direction is one of the factors that has made putting so much more important competitively than it once was.

Wide-open, rough-free golf courses with huge, level, easy-to-hit, easy-to-hold greens are certainly easy to conceive and often to construct; and if you can build these tracks long enough you can generally kid many of the people into thinking they're experiencing a "championship" test. But to me that kind of course takes all the fun out of golf; it destroys the shot-making values and thereby the game's intrinsic challenge. Golf under these circumstances becomes just a game of thumping and putting. No finesse. No need for thought. Just two or three whacks and then out with the putter. On courses like these the best putters are bound to have an advantage over the best shot-makers.

I'd rather have the old type of course—the British-type course—that offers a varied but balanced shot-making challenge from tee to green. That's why I am so proud of my contribution to the Harbour Town golf course on Hilton Head Island in South Carolina. It may have a couple too many gimmicks, but I believe it strikes an unusually fine balance between the shots through the air and the shots along the ground. It helps to re-establish some of the old perspectives. I am certainly striving to do just that in most of the new courses I'm now designing, especially the New Course at Muirfield in Columbus, Ohio, which to date represents my best effort as a golf architect.

It's probably because I feel this way that I putt best on well-contoured, relatively small, fast-running greens such as those at Merion, Pebble Beach, and most of the older championship courses in the United States. I'm at my worst on large, level, slow, turf-nursery-type greens. Frankly, I can't stand 'em! I just don't seem to be able to get "up" for them, which is a factor that in recent years has increasingly influenced my playing schedule. I believe Ben Hogan once said: "If the tees and fairways are in bad shape I'll play, but if the greens are lousy I don't start." I know just how he felt.

However, I'm getting too much into philosophy when my main purpose here is to talk about putting technique. To bring us back on track, and to give you my overview on putting mechanics quickly, let me retell a story I told in a previous book concerning nine holes I once played with my wife, Barbara. We don't often get out on the golf course together, but I'll remember this particular nine holes forever. Just about every time Barbara hit the ball with the putter it went into the hole. And she did it with an awkward stance, faulty alignment, a spread grip with her right thumb off the shaft, and a fast, backswing followed by a jerky forward stroke on which her head bobbed up as the blade bounced off the turf before striking the ball.

Such is putting! Two percent technique, 98 percent inspiration or confidence or "touch"—or luck, Mrs. Nicklaus!

If you gather from this that putting is the least scientific or mechanized part of my game, you'd be right. Beyond a few basic personal keys, mainly related to alignment and tempo, much of what I said earlier in this book about sticking to fundamentals through thick and thin goes out the window the moment I walk onto the green. I will do just about anything to make a putt drop. I'll change my setup or stroke, not only from day to day but from green to green—even from putt to putt. Obviously some of these changes are dictated by course conditions and the slope or speed of the putt at hand. But the majority are purely method adjustments: a searching and experimenting for a certain alignment, or a particular stroking pattern, or a quality of tempo. A good example of how chameleon-like I can become on the greens was the 1972 L. & M.-sponsored PGA Match Play Championship at the Country Club of North Carolina. The stance I used in beating Frank Beard in the final was about the fifth I'd used that summer, and the stroke about the fifteenth.

Don't get the impression from this that I lack confidence in my putting. The real reason for all my fiddling around is that I really do believe what I said with respect to Barbara's miraculous streak—that putting is inspirational, not mechanical. I believe that the outstanding golfers of the past prove this. A few of them were *great* putters, but all were very *good* putters—don't you ever believe a fellow who wins a big tournament and then tells you he wasn't putting worth a darn. Yet, if you look back over their styles, you'll find massive conflict of method. Not one appears to have putted the same way as another.

And this variation of style has never been truer than it is today. Lee Trevino, Billy Casper and Bob Charles, to name just three greats, putt entirely differently one from the other. Lee employs his wrists and forearms to produce a very flowing stroking action. Billy picks the club up with a wrist break and "pops" the ball. Bob putts stiff-wristed, swinging his arms from his shoulder sockets.

The only thing these great putters have in common is "touch," and that's the critical ingredient. But it is my view that none of them found it through "mechanizing" a stroke, nor do I believe they could retain it that way. When you see them out on the practice green before or after a tournament round I suspect that very infrequently will they be trying to "groove" anything. Rather, they will be seeking to heighten their sense of "touch," by constantly adjusting and modifying the various elements of their setup, stroke, and—most of all— the rhythm of their movement.

Essentially, therefore, I regard putting touch as something that's here today, gone tomorrow, back the next day. Which reminds me, I've been meaning to ask Barbara about that split-handed grip of hers. Or maybe it's the way she bounces the club off the green. . . .

THE CONFIDENCE FACTORS

I hope to know a lot more about putting by 1982. Maybe by then I might feel qualified to write a book about it; at the moment I don't. Therefore, as with the other departments of the short game, all I'm going to attempt to cover here are those areas of putting that seem particularly important to me at this time.

The first of these concerns attitude. Most makable putts are missed because of fear or a negative attitude, not because of faulty technique per se. It doesn't take much technique to roll a 1.68-inch ball along a smooth, level surface into, or in the immediate vicinity of, a 4¼-inch hole. With no pressure on you, you could do it one-handed most of the time. But there is *always* pressure on the shorter putts, even when you're just playing around the course alone. That's because a short putt—a "makable" putt—is golf's "last chance" shot. You still have a chance to recover from every other missed stroke. You don't from a short putt. If you miss a 3-footer, it's a stroke gone forever. There is also the problem that you know you *should* make these putts. This brings forth a psychological fear of embarrassment should you miss.

Thus confidence has to be the golfer's greatest single weapon on the greens. If he believes he can get the ball into the hole, a lot of the time he will, even if his technique appears to be unorthodox or even downright faulty. If he doesn't believe he can get the ball into the hole, most of the time he won't, even though his technique may seem flawless.

The widely varying styles of top golfers would seem to prove that putting is far more a matter of "touch," or inspiration, than mechanics. These three superb putters, for example, favor totally different stroking actions. Lee Trevino (top) is an arm-wrist putter; Bill Casper (left) uses virtually a wrists-only action; and Bob Charles is a solid-wristed, arm-shoulder stroker.

"Thanks, Jack," I can hear you say. "Now tell me where to go buy my next year's supply of putting confidence." I wish I knew myself—I'd be first in line. But if I don't know where to buy it I certainly know how to develop it, and I'll be happy to tell you.

The first requirement for confident putting is the ability to read greens: to be able to judge very accurately where and at what speed the ball must roll to reach the hole. For example, if you had played all over the United States you would know that grass in Florida grows toward the setting sun, in California toward the ocean, and in most other parts of the country toward water or away from mountains. You would know that when a bent or Bermuda grass green looks shiny the grain is with you, and when it looks dull or dirty the grain is against you. Obviously experience is a big factor here. But I believe that in gaining knowledge of putting surfaces it becomes more important to look at situations objectively and analytically rather than emotionally. This is just another way of saying *concentrate,* which I believe anyone can do if he or she has enough desire to play well.

The second confidence requirement is the ability to aim the ball where you've decided it should go. This is mechanical, a matter of proper setup alignment that can be learned by anyone who will give a little time and thought to the matter.

The third confidence requirement is the ability to repeatedly stroke the ball in a way that transmits a feeling of fluid, yet solid, contact from the clubface to the hands. This may be partly mechanics, and it is certainly heavily

A HEAD-STEADYING GIMMICK

Probably the premier technical cause of missed putts—especially short putts—is head movement. If you're a congenital head-mover on the forward swing, as many amateurs are, try this: As you stroke through the ball, consciously keep your left shoulder low and still. Don't let it lift even the slightest little bit until the ball is well on its way.

This little gimmick will encourage your hands and arms to traverse the ball correctly, and it will also teach you to follow the putt by swiveling, rather than raising, your head.

influenced by tempo and rhythm, but it is mainly a matter of instinctive "touch." Some people seem to be born with good "touch"—I think I was blessed with a reasonable share. But if you don't have it naturally, I'm afraid the only way you're going to get some is through practice.

THE CLUB

I've used the same putter for more than eleven of my thirteen years as a professional, but I regret to say that if you buy an identical club you'll find that it has no magical properties. Mine's a very ordinary putter. All I can tell you about it technically is that it's of medium weight, is fairly upright in lie, has a square-fronted leather grip and has a flanged blade with two lines across the top that I personally put there to indicate the sweet spot and now use to help in lining up.

I used this putter during my early years on tour, experimented with others for eighteen months, and then reverted back to it. The reason I've stuck to it so loyally is simply that I feel more confident with it than with any other putter I've tried.

"Feel" has got to be the final arbiter in your selection of a putter. If a club feels good, stick with it, whether it's the newest-fangled thing on the market or came out of Uncle Fred's attic. There are no hard-and-fast rules about what constitutes a good putter, any more than there are about what constitutes a good putting method.

There are, however, a few technical points worth bearing in mind in selecting a putter. It should place your hands in a comfortable position when soled flat behind the ball. Thus, if you putt best with an upright method and your hands high—the style of most good putters on tour does seem to be fairly upright—then get a putter with an upright lie. But if you perform best with a flatter stroke, match the lie of your putter to that method.

Before you buy a putter, locate the "sweet spot" (I believe "percussion point" is the technical term) and decide if it's where you want it to be. You can find the sweet spot easily by bouncing a ball along the putter face while holding it horizontally. When you feel no vibration in the shaft, the ball is bouncing on the sweet spot. I like a putter with its sweet spot right in the center of the blade, because that's where I instinctively will tend to meet the ball and where consciously I try to do so. But you'll find that most putters have the sweet spot closer to the heel.

Weight also can be a significant factor in putter selection. On tour we encounter so many speeds of greens that if I had a putter for all of them, I'd have no room in the trunk for the rest of my clubs. I compromise by using a medium-weight club, but if your home course greens are consistently fast, then you might do better with a light putter. If they're slow, a heavier putter might serve you better.

Another factor to consider here is your stroke. If it tends to get too fast, a heavier putter might improve your tempo. But if you're a hesitant stroker with a tendency to quit at the ball, a lighter putter might force you to accelerate your forward stroke.

In the final analysis, though, don't worry too much about the minor technicalities. Go with the putter that feels best, because it's the one that will inspire the greatest confidence in you.

THE GRIP

To me, the putting stroke is basically a right-handed action; the left hand guides the club while the right does the stroking or hitting. Thus I favor the reverse-overlap grip—the forefinger of the left hand laying over the fingers of the right hand—because it places all four fingers of my right hand on the club. Another reason I like this grip is that it helps me to place my right hand directly behind the shaft with the palm parallel to the putterface, so that when I push my right hand squarely toward the hole the putterface must also move in that direction. Yet another reason I prefer the reverse-overlap grip is that, after using it for twenty years, it feels supremely comfortable, and comfort over the ball is imperative in putting.

I hold the club in the same place on the shaft for all putts, but my grip pressure varies depending on the type of stroke I am using. Generally you could describe it as easy to firm—rarely loose and certainly never tight.

I hold the putter predominantly in my fingers, with both thumbs set straight down the square top of the grip. The back of my left hand is turned very slightly to face a bit left of target. This helps prevent any tendency to turn the club in that direction on the forward swing and thus pull the ball. There is a firmness in the pressure of my left thumb on the top of the club that I feel helps to create a center point or fulcrum for the stroke. My chief "touch" finger is the right forefinger, and I curl it onto the club in such a way that its middle knuckle points down centrally between my heels. This is a safeguard against pulling or pushing the ball off-line with a finger that does much of the hitting. If my right forefinger were wrapped on the club so that this knuckle pointed to the outside of my right heel, I'd tend to pull the ball; if it pointed to my left heel, I'd push the ball.

I owe a lot to Jack Burke, now at Champions Club in Houston but a

At a guess, I'd say that at least 80 percent of top professional and amateur golfers today use the reverse-overlap putting grip. My chief reason for having used this grip throughout my career is that I putt primarily with my right hand, and the reverse-overlap is conducive to right-handed control because it places all the fingers of that hand on the club.

prominent tournament player when I first joined the tour, for my grip position, especially that of the right hand. Jack was always a super putter, so when I played a practice round with him in the winter of 1962 I took the opportunity to ask for some help on my then-ailing stroke. Jack felt that my problem lay in a tendency to pull the putter into the ball with my fingers, instead of pushing it through with my right palm. He suggested I place my right hand turned farther to the right, so that the thumb rested on top of the shaft and the palm was placed directly behind the shaft in a strong, yet square, pushing position. I did as he advised and my putting improved, and I've stuck with this right-hand grip ever since.

There are a zillion ways to hold a putter. I don't think it matters much which one a golfer adopts, so long as it is comfortable, promotes a square-bladed swing through the ball, and is conducive to smooth rhythm.

THE SETUP

You may have noticed at tournaments or on TV how meticulously I align myself for all shots, and you'll no doubt recall how deeply I went into this area of the game when discussing full shots earlier. Common sense would seem to indicate that the smaller the target, the more important aim and alignment become. Thus, in putting, aim and alignment reach a zenith of importance.

Perhaps the most dramatic example of their importance in my career occurred in the 1966 Masters. On the seventy-first green I missed an almost straight 3-foot putt—it didn't even touch the hole. Later I happened to see myself stroking that putt on TV. The camera was looking directly down the line of the putt, catching me in profile. The reason I'd missed it hit me like a kick in the teeth. My head was bent so far over that my eyes were positioned *beyond* the ball, outside the target line. Thus they were giving me an incorrect visual impression of the line. By aligning the putter to the line my eyes saw, I had given myself no chance of making that putt. I went immediately to the practice green, confirmed the fault, and did enough corrective work on it to win a playoff the next day against Tommy Jacobs and Gay Brewer.

Stance and posture in putting are to me relatively insignificant, so long as one is comfortable and therefore relaxed and stable. But it is my conviction that, to putt well, your eyes must be either vertically over the ball, or vertically over the ball-target line behind (to the right of) the ball. If your eyes are not so positioned, I believe you will be misled by your optical impressions into aiming the clubface erroneously, and thus to misdirecting the ball. In my case, the erroneous line I "see" if I position my eyes outside of the ball-target line is to the left of the hole, and I miss the putt to that side of the cup by aiming the putter face in that direction. Conversely, if my eyes are inside the ball-target line, the erroneous line I see is to the right of the hole, and I aim and miss right.

I believe that all great, and most good, putters conform to the principle of positioning their eyes directly over either the ball or the ball-target line, whether they know it or not. On tour the majority of players certainly seem to set up with their eyes directly over the ball. Personally, over the years I've gone from that position, to having my eyes over the ball-target line but well back of the ball, to again being directly over the ball, then back again, stopping for various spells at just about each point en route. Today, I still often readjust my eye positioning slightly, depending on the type of stroke I'm trying to make. But basically I seem now to have settled for positioning my eyes well back of, rather than directly over, the ball. The reason is that this eye position, combined with my bent-over, almost crouching stance, enables me to feel that I can "see" my line running through and well out beyond the ball—just as a sharpshooter peers from his eye through the rifle sight out to his target. On short putts particularly this type of sighting is helpful, in that I can actually *see* the cup in my peripheral vision as I stroke the ball.

What other aspects of setup are important?

I've mentioned comfort and stability, but should perhaps add that the main reason these are so important is to prevent head and body movement. You can stroke with your wrists alone, as Arnold Palmer and Billy Casper largely do, or with your arms alone, as do Bob Charles and George Archer, or with your wrists and arms, as Lee Trevino and I do. But nobody I've ever come across—except Barbara!—can putt with a swaying head and upper-body motion.

I believe that stance and body alignment are best dictated by the demands of comfort and stability, which are largely matters of personal preference. I set up pretty squarely to the line of the putt in my feet and body most of the time, chiefly because it seems the natural thing to do and I feel comfortable that way. But I'll modify my stance to suit my mood at any time, even in the middle of a round.

One very important setup point is the alignment of the putter shaft. I believe you can putt effectively setting it at the vertical at address, as I do, or with it angled slightly toward the target (in which case you might need a putter with a little loft on the face to offset the delofting effect of the hands being forward).

WHEN "SPOT" PUTTING CAN HELP

I'm not normally a "spot" putter. I see an imaginary over-all line in my mind, rather than a specific mark in the grass over which to hit the ball. But spot putting can help. If you're missing the short ones, select a specific spot 2 or 3 inches in front of the hole, and try to make the ball run over it. I think such a tiny target is more specific than the 4¼-inch hole itself, and thus it forces you to line up and stroke more precisely.

GOLF MY WAY
Jack Nicklaus

Most good putters on the professional tour seem to set up with their eyes directly over the ball. I've positioned myself thus at times, but generally I prefer to set my eyes over the ball—target line but well back of the ball (left). This way I get the feeling that I can "see" my line running through and well out beyond the ball. On short putts I can actually see the cup with my peripheral vision as I make my stroke. Other stance factors concern me less, so long as I feel comfortable, well-balanced and relaxed.

But I believe it is very difficult to putt well with the hands *behind* the clubhead at address. Reasons? First, you'll be likely to stub the putterhead on the ground going back. Second, to avoid doing that, you'll instinctively tend to lift the putterhead up high on the backswing and, as a consequence, chop down on the ball coming forward.

When I first joined the professional tour, 1956 Masters champion Jack Burke gave me a putting lesson that is still paying dividends. Jack modified my right-hand position so that my palm paralleled the clubface, then told me to simply push the hand squarely in whichever direction I wanted the ball to roll. In practice, I constantly check that my right hand is in position to push the club directly along the target line. If it moves under or over the shaft, invariably I will begin to push putts to the right or pull them to the left.

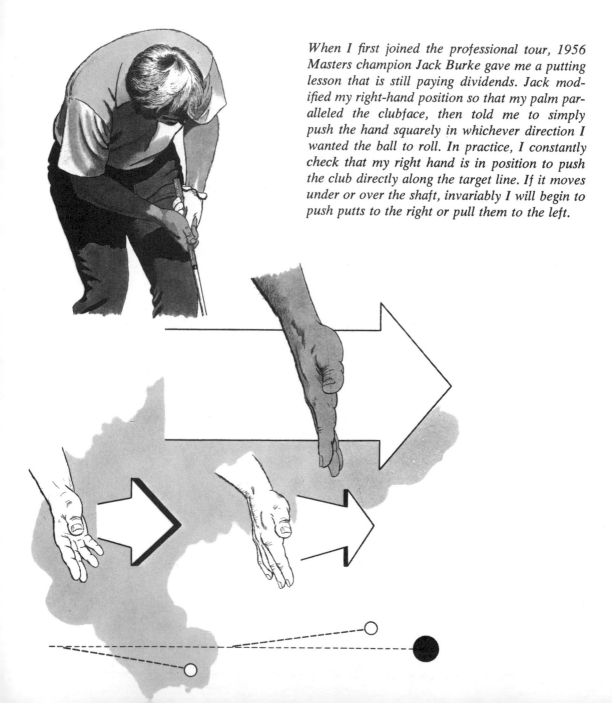

Ball position is important only in the sense that you should locate the ball in relation to your feet where you can best swing the putterhead squarely through it, low enough to the ground to meet the back of the ball solidly. For me that ball position is normally opposite my left toe on a level putt. Putting uphill I might move the ball forward a little, and back a little putting downhill. But for other golfers my positions might not be ideal. You must experiment to discover what works best for you.

Depending on what type of stroke you use, a significant factor in putting can be the positioning of your elbows. I use my right elbow as a sort of guide, in a pistonlike action, during the stroke, and I can best do this when it remains close to my right side. Thus I position it there at address. So far as the left elbow is concerned, I've never been really sure whether it should be very close to, or a little away from, the left side. I do know, however, that when I have held my left elbow away from my side it has usually been easier for me to keep my left hand and arm moving toward the hole on the forward stroke.

Until about three years ago I would always aim putts by aiming the club-face, squaring it to the line along which I wanted the ball to start rolling. During the time I was experimenting with putters, however, one of the clubs I used was a Ping, which had two little lines cut into the center top of the blade at right angles to it. I must have thought they were helpful because I added two similar lines to my old putter when I reverted to it. But then for years I continued to aim with the clubface, virtually ignoring the lines I'd made. Then about three years ago I suddenly started aiming with the lines instead of the putterface— don't ask me why. It must have helped me at the time, because I'm still doing it today. But in putting you never know; next week, if something goes wrong, I might be back aiming with the clubface again.

THE STROKE

I remember once writing that I was a "square to square" putter. Well, I've learned a couple of things since then, among them the advantages of using different types of stroke for different moods and situations. Today I am some-times a square-to-square putter, I am sometimes an open-to-closed putter, and I am sometimes a closed-to-open putter. And I couldn't tell you which it will be from week to week.

For example, in the 1972 Masters I was an open-to-closed putter, simply because that's the way I felt I could putt best that April. Earlier in the year, playing in the Eastern Airlines-Doral Open, I'd also been an open-to-closed putter, because I felt that this type of stroke would most effectively start and

PRACTICE TO A TEE

Instead of practicing to an actual hole, try putting to a tee stuck in the ground. By making you less "cup conscious," this will help you concentrate better on speed and line, and thus on tempo and stroke pattern. I often use this training technique even for short-putt practice. Once I get onto the course, the hole looks like a bucket.

keep the ball rolling along the top of the spiky Bermuda grass greens. But then in June, at Pebble Beach in the U. S. Open, I became a closed-to-open putter, partly because that was the action that seemed to be working best, and partly because the greens were lightning fast and tricky and I felt the need for a "gentler" contact. The next month, at the British Open on Muirfield's smooth, true, but not unduly fast greens, I was a square-to-square putter, as I was later on the fine greens of the Country Club of North Carolina in the L. & M. PGA Match Play Championship. But in between those two events, I'd been an open-to-closed putter in the Westchester Classic. Since I won all but one of those tournaments, each method obviously had its merits as far as I was concerned at the time.

What are the differences among them? Well, they're really very slight.

When I'm putting square-to-square, I endeavor to swing the clubface away from and back through the ball without its face ever turning. When I'm putting open-to-closed, which I usually reserve for poor or slow or heavily grained greens, I allow the clubface to rotate slightly clockwise on the backswing and commensurately counterclockwise through the ball. (If the greens are very bad, I'll often combine this open-to-closed action with striking the top half of the ball, to promote overspin even more.) My closed-to-open stroke is just the reverse of the open-to-closed action: The clubface rotates a little counter-clockwise going back and a little clockwise going through, producing a soft or gentle sort of impact.

This is subtle stuff, of course, and I don't intend that the once-a-week golfer should immediately go out and try to adopt such methods. My recommendation to him would be to stick with a square-to-square-type stroke until he has mastered the art of consistently striking the ball solidly on the putter's sweet spot. I describe my own variations simply to emphasize again that

I do not believe that it is optically possible for the normally sighted person to attain a correct visual impression of the line of a putt at address unless his eyes are positioned directly above the ball–target line. If the eyes are positioned inside this line, the putting line "seen" will actually go to the right of the hole. If the eyes are outside the ball–target line, the seemingly correct putting line will actually go left of the hole.

"touch" or "feel" is so much more the key to putting than mere mechanics.

Whatever my clubface manipulation the basic components of my actual putting stroke generally remain pretty standard. As an amateur I was a fairly stiff-wristed putter, but as I began to play a greater variety of courses after turning professional I found I could not consistently make solid contact with the ball with this rather "wooden" method. I felt I lacked "touch." Thus I went for a while to the other extreme—an all-wrist stroke. In recent years that has been modified into my present wrist-arm stroking action.

Arm putters generally take the club back with the left hand in command, then hit the ball with the right hand. Like most wrist or arm-and-wrist putters, I take the club back with my right hand, and I hit the ball with my right hand, with the left hand acting primarily as a guide and as a sort of fulcrum for the hinging of the wrists.

Since my putter is almost vertical at address, I can swing it on short and medium-length putts pendulumlike, pretty much on line throughout the stroke. On long putts, of course, the club must move inside the target line on the backswing and inside again on the follow-through. I do not make a conscious effort to keep the club low to the ground on the backswing—although I don't pick it up, either—but I do sometimes strive to keep it low and on line going out and after the ball.

My overriding objective in putting is to develop a feeling of fluidity, yet firmness, at impact between my hands and the clubface, which tells me I am striking the ball truly and solidly. The key to this sensation lies far less in the mechanics of the stroke than in its tempo.

Thus for the sake of tempo more than anything else, I belong to the stroking rather than to the rapping or popping school of thought. My objective is not to "hit" the ball, but to swing the putter back with my wrists and forearms at a slow and deliberate tempo, and then swing it *through* the ball at *exactly the same tempo* with a reciprocating wrist-forearm motion.

Consequently, the length of the backswing is the factor that primarily controls the force of my putting stroke. Before the 1971 PGA Championship Deane Beman gave me a lesson about getting the putter back before bringing it forward, and it improved my putting 100 percent. Since then I've been particularly concerned about making an adequate backswing relative to the distance I want to roll the ball.

One final point that probably needs clarification in relation to my emphasis on the function of the right hand in my stroke is that, although the right hand does most of the work, the left hand must always work in close unison with it, particularly on the through stroke. Also, if the left hand checks or quits at any point before contact, it will have a blocking effect on the right hand's action. That will disrupt the swing path, or the clubface alignment, or both.

PRACTICE

I practice putting in four ways.

When my stroke goes sour, I work on it—usually after a tournament round or at home—by hitting balls, with little concern as to where they go. My total concern is with tempo and solid contact. Once I have hit, say, ten putts consecutively at the tempo and with the contact feel I'm seeking between my hands and the clubface, I quit. I know I can't "mechanize" or "groove" that

Although my putting posture varies, most of the time I bend comparatively low over the ball in an almost crouched position, with my right shoulder considerably lower than my left. This posture enables me to use my right forearm almost like a piston, moving it back and forward on an almost horizontal path. I find this an excellent way to add power to the stroke on long putts without increasing wrist action to a point where I would excessively lift and lower the putterhead.

particular stroke forever, and that by going on longer I could lose immediately whatever "touch" I'd just developed. Thus I always stop when I feel I've achieved my objective, even though I know my success may be temporary.

My second form of putting practice consists of fairly frequent half-hour sessions when I am at home, checking out and tuning up my grip, setup, stroke, tempo, etc.

I do my third type of putting practice before each tournament round. Here I stroke the ball to a definite target, but with the prime objective of relating the tempo and mechanics of the stroke to the conditions I'll find on the golf course. I am, you might say, "feeling out" the greens as they are that day, and also my metabolism of the moment, and trying to harmonize the two. Usually I'll start by loosening up with a few middle-distance putts. Then I'll stroke a few long ones to measure how well I'm judging distance. Most of the time, though, I will work from about 15 feet down to about 4 feet—the "makable" putt range. Such a session rarely lasts more than ten minutes. I'll quit as soon as I feel satisfied that I've matched my stroke to the speed or texture of the greens, even if I've only been out there two minutes. I have never believed in wasting putts on practice greens.

My fourth type of putting practice happens on the golf course itself. In making practice swings with the putter I never just wave it around to ease my nerves or kill time. With each practice stroke I try to simulate the exact feel of the upcoming putt in terms of rhythm and length of swing. In short, I simultaneously measure and rehearse the real thing through my very deliberate practice swings.

If you've never had a set plan for putting practice, may I recommend the above to you wholeheartedly—especially the fourth aspect of it. You might find that such a positive attitude on practice strokes greatly boosts your ability to concentrate, as well as your ability to hole putts.

There are a few more points on putting practice that you might find helpful if you don't already employ them. First, avoid practicing too much on any one type of green, or any one type of putt. Even on the same course, greens vary from day to day, and you need to be able to handle the variations. So switch your practice locations and angles. Second, remember that distance is more difficult to judge than direction in putting. So practice speed more than accuracy. Third, stress practicing the putts that you can reasonably expect to make. Lagging a few long putts during every session is valuable in judging distance, and it will give you a good reading of the tempo of your stroke, but it is on putts from 12 feet and less that you are looking to hole out. That is where practice will pay the greatest dividends.

There it is then; the Jack Nicklaus putting method as I write these words. But if you see me doing something entirely different out there next week, don't be surprised. Remember, I'll do *anything* to make a putt.

Endpiece

One aspect of my personality that has at times helped my career, and at others brought me a lot of heartache, is my desire for perfection in all things. I hate to do *anything* less well than I believe it can be done, and most of all I hate to play golf less well than I think it can be played.

Of course, I never have played golf perfectly, and there is a mighty good chance that neither I nor anyone else ever will. But that doesn't mean to say I won't go on trying to for as long as I feel I have some chance of meeting that goal.

With the exception of one three-year period (1967–70), I feel I have become a better golfer every year since I took up the game at ten years of age. The better I have become, the more I have embarrassed myself by my failures; and the more I have embarrassed myself, the more I have been goaded into trying to develop greater skills. Of this I am presently certain: When failure ceases to embarrass me, and thus to stimulate me to greater efforts, my day will be done and I shall quit playing golf in public.

How would I define perfection in golf? What to me would represent a flawless performance?

If I could achieve 100 percent in everything, on a par-72 course I would shoot birdies on the fourteen par-3 and par-4 holes, and eagles on the four par-5 holes. That would give me an eighteen-hole score of 50, and four such rounds in a seventy-two-hole tournament would be 200.

Since the best single round ever scored on a championship course on the PGA tour is listed as 60, and my best-ever eighteen-hole competitive round is 62, and since the best-ever major championship winning score for 72 holes is 271 (that records happens to be mine), you can see that the entire golfing world, including me, has a lot of target to shoot for before anyone ever plays 100 percent golf.

That's one reason why the flame of incentive can always burn high.

As I see it, three elements are involved in playing perfect golf. First I would have to have achieved 100 percent analytical objectivity—recognized the ideal shot for each situation. Second, having recognized the perfect shot, I would have to have resolved to play it—no compromises. Third, having recognized and resolved to play the perfect shot, I would have to have executed it perfectly—no technical hitches.

My highest rate of failure occurs, of course, in execution. Maturity and experience have brought me to a point where, when I'm concentrating properly, objective shot analysis presents few major problems. How much I compromise depends on my confidence level, but when it's high I can be pretty resolute about attempting the proper shot. In terms of execution, I feel the nearest I've ever got to the goals I've set myself is about 75 percent. At my worst, I probably do not reach 33 percent. Over-all, day in and day out, at the present time I'm probably averaging about 60 percent.

Which shots most often trip me? Well, let's run quickly through the bag and take a look.

DRIVER.   Power has always been my greatest asset, but never so much as it is today. The reason is that in the last two or three years I have become a reasonably straight as well as a long driver. Also, I can now drive the ball low, and move it at will either from left to right or from right to left off the tee. Thus I'd put my driving at, say, 85 percent.

FAIRWAY WOODS.   I've also become a slightly better fairway wood player these past two or three years, but—as my record on long par-5 holes shows, particularly in the Masters at Augusta—my three-wood play is still comparatively weak. The reason is simple enough: I'm not called upon to use the club much in tournament play; thus I don't practice it as much as I ought to. Currently I'd rate this area of my game at no better than 65 percent.

LONG IRONS.   By and large, my long-iron play is pretty good. Sure, I'll miss shots from time to time, but over-all I'm happy with my long irons. I'd rate myself here at about 90 percent.

MIDDLE IRONS.   Here, again, I'm content in the sense that my percentage of misses is small and I can play a wide variety of middle-iron shots. Thus again I'd mark myself at 90 percent.

SHORT IRONS.   Obviously, the shorter the shot the tighter one's targets become and thus the greater the percentage for error. Nevertheless, I'm not happy with my short-iron play. I'm better in this area than I was three years ago, but I still lack the finesse—the total ball control—that I think I should have. There are still shots I can't play with complete confidence, especially with the wedges. Thus here I would be hard pressed to give myself much better than 50 percent.

CHIPPING.   I've improved at chipping recently by practicing it more than I used to, but it's still definitely a weak link in my armor. The reason, again, is that I don't miss a lot of greens, thus don't get to chip the ball a lot under competitive conditions. I'd mark myself currently at about 60 percent as a chipper.

BUNKER SHOTS.   My bunker play tends to be in and out, depending a lot on the type of sand I'm playing from. Generally, however, this area of my game has improved considerably, to the point where—especially when I'm playing from sand I like—I'd say I was a pretty good trap player. Rating: 80 percent in firm sand, nearer 50 percent in powdery or silica sand.

PUTTING.   Putting has always been an in-and-out game for me, depending a great deal on how well I'm concentrating and, to a lesser extent, on the type of greens I'm playing. For example, I've never putted as well on slow greens as on fast. But you have to be realistic about putting, and accept the fact that you're probably never going to putt as well as you think you ought to. Realistically, I'd rate my putting somewhere between 70 and 80 percent on an over-all basis, with lows of about 30 percent and occasional highs of about 90 percent.

Quite obviously there is considerable room for improvement in the Nicklaus golf game, and you can be sure that every effort is being made to effect it. Given my present health, I believe that I can continue to sharpen and improve my game in the physical sense for at least another five years. How well this is reflected by my performances over that period is almost entirely a matter of desire. At the moment, I have that in spades.

I hope you've enjoyed this book, and I hope something herein helps you with your own golf game.

In my experience, when all is said and done, success at golf boils down to four pretty straightforward factors. First I would place adherence to a few time-proven mechanical fundamentals and a resistance to the passing gimmick. Second, I think a vital—and often overlooked—success factor is how effectively a golfer can maximize his greatest natural physical assets in molding and maintaining a playing method. Third, I would select the ability while playing to define objectives and then to concentrate on achieving them to the exclusion of all else. Fourth, and most important of all, there is the matter of desire. If you have enough of that it's amazing what you can do at golf, or in any other area of life, for that matter.

Career Records

Personalia

- Born January 21, 1940, in Columbus, Ohio.
- Height 5 feet 11½ inches. Weight 185 pounds.
- Married to the former Barbara Bash July 23, 1960.
- Five children: Jack William II, Steven Charles, Nancy Jean, Gary Thomas, Michael Scott

AMATEUR CAREER HIGHLIGHTS

At age 10   Carded 51 for first nine holes ever played.

At age 13   Played in first national tournament (USGA Junior Championship for ages eighteen and under), winning first three matches before being eliminated. Won Ohio State Junior Championship and Columbus Junior Match Play Championship.

At age 14   Captured Stroke Play and Match Play Columbus Junior Championships.

At age 15   Again won both above titles and also Columbus Amateur Championship. Qualified for U. S. Amateur Championship for first time, losing in first round.

At age 16   Won Ohio State Open (seventy-two-hole stroke-play event) against strong field, with final rounds of 64-72. Also won Ohio State Junior title and lost National Jaycees Championship in playoff.

At age 17   Won National Jaycees Championship. Qualified for first time for U. S. Open, missing cut.

At age 18   Won Trans-Mississippi Championship. Qualified for U. S. Open, making cut and finishing in tie for forty-first place. Playing in first PGA tour event (Rubber City Open at Firestone), was one stroke out of lead at halfway point with rounds of 67 and 66; finished with 76-68 for twelfth spot.

At age 19   Won 1959 U. S. Amateur Championship, defeating Charles Coe 1-up in thirty-six-hole final at Broadmoor, Colorado Springs. Played for first time on winning U. S. Walker Cup team against Britain at Muirfield, Scotland. Won North-South and Trans-Mississippi championships.

At age 20   Second to Arnold Palmer in U. S. Open by 2 strokes at Cherry Hills, Denver, establishing a record 282 for an amateur in the Open. Individual winner in World Amateur Team Championship by 13 strokes with 269, eclipsing Ben Hogan's record by 18 shots at Merion Cricket Club, Haverford, Pennsylvania.

At age 21   In last year as amateur won second U. S. Amateur Championship, defeating Dudley Wysong 8 and 6 at Pebble Beach, California. Member of winning U. S. Walker Cup team. Western Amateur champion; NCAA champion.

PROFESSIONAL CAREER IN CAPSULE

(through 1973)

Official tour victories	51
Second place or ties	34
Third place or ties	25

Career Winnings through 1973 (official tour money): $2,289,954

Top Money Winner, 1964, 1965, 1967, 1971, 1972, 1973 (also runner-up twice, third three times, and fourth once in eleven pro years)

PGA Player of the Year Award, 1967, 1972, 1973

"Major championship" titles, 14: Masters (4); U. S. Open (3); PGA Championship (3); British Open (2); U. S. Amateur (2).

International Victories:

British Open (2): 1966, 1970 (runner-up four times)
Australian Open (3): 1964, 1968, 1971
World Cup: winner of individual championship a record three times (1963, 1964, 1971) and six times a member of winning U.S. teams (1963, 1964, 1966, 1967, 1971, 1973)
Ryder Cup: member of U.S. teams ever since eligible (1969, 1971, 1973)

MAJOR CHAMPIONSHIP RECORD

YEAR	MASTERS	U. S. OPEN	PGA CHAMPIONSHIP	BRITISH OPEN
1962	Tied 15th	Won	Tied 3rd	Tied 32nd
1963	Won	Missed cut	Won	3rd
1964	Tied 2nd	Tied 23rd	Tied 2nd	2nd
1965	Won	Tied 31st	Tied 2nd	Tied 12th
1966	Won	3rd	Tied 22nd	Won
1967	Missed cut	Won	Tied 3rd	2nd
1968	Tied 5th	2nd	Missed cut	Tied 2nd
1969	Tied 24th	Tied 25th	Tied 11th	Tied 6th
1970	8th	Tied 49th	Tied 6th	Won
1971	Tied 2nd	2nd	Won	Tied 5th
1972	Won	Won	Tied 13th	2nd
1973	Tied 3rd	Tied 4th	Won	4th
TOTAL	Won four	Won three	Won three	Won twice
	2nd twice	2nd twice	2nd twice	2nd four times
	3rd once	3rd once	3rd twice	3rd once

PROFESSIONAL CAREER HIGHLIGHTS YEAR BY YEAR

1962 Highlights

Official tour victories and winnings at each:

U. S. Open	$15,000
Seattle Open	4300
Portland Open	3500

Runner-up in three tournaments, third four times.
Official winnings for year: $61,868.95 for third place.

- Won $33.33 in first professional tournament, the Los Angeles Open.
- Won the World Series of Golf eight months later, earning $50,000.
- Won first pro title, defeating Arnold Palmer in playoff for the U. S. Open. Youngest-ever winner of the U. S. Open.
- Won back-to-back tournaments at Seattle and Portland.
- Won money in all twenty-six tournaments entered.
- Named Rookie of the Year for 1962.

Official U.S. tour victories and winnings at each:

Masters	$20,000
PGA Championship	13,000
Tournament of Champions	13,000
Sahara Invitational	13,000
Palm Springs Classic	9000

Runner-up in two tournaments, third three times.
Official winnings for year: $100,040 for second place.

- Won individual championship at World Cup in Paris, teaming with Arnold Palmer to win the event for the United States.
- Again won the World Series of Golf, earning $50,000.
- Became youngest-ever winner of the Masters, by 1 shot over Tony Lema.
- Finished third in British Open after bogeying last two holes.
- Won PGA Championship by 2 strokes.

1964 Highlights

Official U. S. tour victories and winnings at each:

Whitemarsh Open	$24,042
Tournament of Champions	12,000
Phoenix Open	7500
Portland Open	5800

Runner-up in six tournaments, third three times.
Official winnings for year: $113,284.50 for first place.

- Won Australian Open in playoff with Bruce Devlin.
- Won individual championship in World Cup in Hawaii, teaming with Arnold Palmer to win the event for the United States.
- Runner-up in British Open at St. Andrews, breaking record for final thirty-six holes with 66-68.
- Achieved best stroke average on tour with 69.9.
- Money winnings victory represented a margin of $81.13 over Palmer.

1965 Highlights

Official U.S. tour victories and winnings at each:

Masters	$20,000
Philadelphia Classic	24,300
Thunderbird Classic	20,000
Memphis Open	9000
Portland Open	6600

Runner-up in four tournaments, third twice.
Official winnings for year: $140,752.14 for first place.

- Won money winnings title for second year, with record total.
- Won Masters title with record score of 271, breaking Ben Hogan's 1953 total by 3 strokes. Also tied course record with 64 in third round.
- Achieved top stroke average for second consecutive year with 70.1.
- Won Portland Open for third time and Philadelphia (Whitemarsh) title second year in a row.
- Took second place in World Series of Golf and also in the individual World Cup honors in Madrid.

1966 Highlights

Official U.S. tour victories and winnings at each:

Masters	$20,000
Sahara Invitational	20,000
National Team Championship (with Arnold Palmer)	25,000

Runner-up in three tournaments, third three times.
Official winnings for year: $111,419.16 for second place.

- Won British Open at Muirfield, Scotland, becoming the fourth and youngest golfer to win the four major titles (Masters, U. S. Open, PGA, British Open.)
- Became the first back-to-back winner of the Masters after a playoff with Tommy Jacobs and Gay Brewer.
- With Arnold Palmer established a team record of 32 under par in National Team Championship.
- Teamed with Arnold Palmer to win the World Cup in Tokyo for the United States.
- Reached the half-million mark in official career winnings.
- After five years as a professional had never finished lower than third in final money standings, and had finished in the money 110 times out of 114 tour starts.

Official U.S. tour victories and winnings at each:

U. S. Open	$30,000
Westchester Classic	50,000
Saraha Invitational	20,000
Western Open	20,000
Crosby National	16,000

Runner-up in two tournaments, third three times.
Official winnings for year: $188,998.08 for first place.

- Sank a 22-foot putt on the final green at Baltusrol to break Ben Hogan's U. S. Open record of 1948 with 275.
- Captured the Professional Player of the Year award in his first year of eligibility as PGA member.
- Finished one shot behind winner at PGA Championship and two behind at British Open.
- Won Sahara event for third time, shooting a career-low round of 62.
- Won the World Series of Golf for the third time.
- Winning $50,000 in World Series, plus the same amount at Westchester, gave him $100,000 in a twelve-day period.
- Set new records in money winnings: $188,998.08 official and $261,566.66 unofficial earnings.
- Teamed with Arnold Palmer to win the World Cup in Mexico City for the fourth time.

1968 Highlights

Official U.S. tour victories and winnings at each:

Western Open	$26,000
American Golf Classic	25,000

Runner-up in three tournaments, third once.
Official winnings for year: $155,285.55 for second place.

- Won Australian Open for second time, setting course record 64 in second round.
- Won longest playoff of year, defeating Lee Elder at fifth hole in American Golf Classic, Frank Beard being eliminated at first extra hole.
- Won back-to-back tournaments at Western Open and American Classic, and tied for second at Westchester, winning $71,416 in three-week period in August.
- Achieved runner-up spot in three national Opens: U.S., Canadian, and British.

1969 Highlights

Official U.S. tour victories and winnings at each:

Andy Williams-	
San Diego Open	$30,000
Kaiser Invitational	28,000
Sahara Invitational	20,000

Runner-up in one tournament.
Official winnings for year: $140,167.42 for third place.

- Approached the million-dollar mark and became second in all-time career earnings with $996,524.17 after eight years as a pro.
- Won the Sahara event for the fourth time.
- Won Kaiser after a sudden-death playoff against three others.
- Late-season surge earned $62,300 in three consecutive events: wins at Sahara and Kaiser and second place in Hawaiian Open.
- By end of season had lost twenty pounds in weight and six inches off hips.

1970 Highlights

Official U.S. tour victories and winnings at each:

Byron Nelson Classic	$20,000
National Team Championship	20,000
(with Arnold Palmer)	

Runner-up in three tournaments, third twice.
Official winnings for year: $142,148 for fourth place.

- Won British Open for second time after eighteen-hole playoff with Doug Sanders at St. Andrews.
- Won World Series of Golf and $50,000 check for a record fourth time.
- Won Piccadilly World Match Play Championship at Wentworth, England.
- Defeated Arnold Palmer on first extra hole in Byron Nelson Classic.
- Teamed with Palmer to win National Team Championship for second time with score of 25 under par.
- Won $76,400 in non-U. S.-tour events.

Official U.S. tour victories and winnings at each:

PGA Championship	$40,000
Tournament of Champions	33,000
Disney World Open	30,000
Byron Nelson Classic	25,000
National Team Championship (with Arnold Palmer)	20,000

Runner-up in three tournaments, third three times.
Official winnings for year: $244,490.50 for first place.

- With victory in the PGA championship, became first golfer to capture the four major championships twice each.
- Established new money winnings record, bringing his official career total to almost $1,400,000.
- Teamed with Arnold Palmer to win the National Team Championship for the third time.
- Won Tournament of Champions for third time (by 8 strokes).
- Late-season surge included four wins in five starts: Australian Open (by 8 strokes); Australian Dunlop (by 7 strokes); World Cup individual honors (by 7 strokes); Disney World Open (by 3 strokes).
- Teamed with Lee Trevino to win the World Cup in Florida for the United States for a record third time.
- Tied Trevino in U. S. Open, losing playoff 68–71.
- Tied for second in Masters, two strokes behind the winner.

1972 Highlights

Official U.S. tour victories and winnings at each:

Bing Crosby	$28,000
Doral Eastern Open	30,000
Masters	25,000
U. S. Open	30,000
Westchester Classic	50,000
U. S. Professional Match Play Championship	40,000
Disney World Open	30,000

Runner-up in three tournaments.
Official winnings for year: $320,542 for first place.

- Finished second in British Open at Muirfield after final round 66, one shot behind Lee Trevino.
- Won $90,000 in a seventeen-day period by taking the Westchester Classic for the second time, and winning his first U. S. Professional Match Play Championship.
- Won seven tournaments out of nineteen U. S. events entered.
- Established new one-year money-winning record of $320,542, bringing his all-time official earnings to $1,981,830.
- Won Masters for fourth time.
- Won U. S. Open for third time.
- Repeated his victory in the Disney World Open with a 19-under-par total of 267, giving him a 9-stroke margin over runner-up Bobby Mitchell.

1973 Highlights

Official U. S. tour victories and winnings at each:

Greater New Orleans Open	$25,000
Bing Crosby	36,000
Atlanta Classic	30,000
Tournament of Champions	40,000
PGA Championship	45,000
Ohio Kings Island Open	25,000
Disney World Open	30,000

Runner-up in one tournament
Official earnings: $308,124 (leading money-winner); first man in golf to surpass $2,000,000 in all-time official earnings.

- Won third PGA Championship.
- Surpassed Bobby Jones' record on August 12 with **PGA Championship** victory, his 14th major championship win.
- Out of seventeen tour events entered in 1973, won seven and finished 15 times in the top ten, 13 times in the top six.
- Finished fourth in the British Open, breaking the Troon course record with a seven-under-par 65 in the final round.
- Won fifty-first U.S. tour victory.
- Teamed with John Miller to win the World Cup in Marbella, Spain for the sixth time.

1974 Highlights

Official U.S. tour victories and winnings at each:

Hawaiian Open	$44,000
Tournament of Champions	50,000

Finished second in The Colonial National and in the PGA Championship.
Official tour earnings: $236,520; all-time official earnings now surpass $2,500,000.

- Out of eighteen tour events entered in 1974, he finished in the top ten 13 times, 8 times in the top six.

1975 Highlights

Official U.S. tour victories and winnings at each:

Doral Eastern Open	$30,000
Heritage Classic	40,000
Masters	40,000
PGA Championship	45,000
World Open	40,000

Runner-up in one tournament.
Official earnings including non-tour events: $330,123; all-time earnings now surpass $2,750,000.

- In non-tour appearances, won the Australian Open.
- Tied with Tom Weiskopf for Canadian Open, lost on first extra hole play-off.
- In nineteen appearances including non-tour events, won six, and finished 17 times in the top ten.
- Shot 30 out of 64 tour rounds in the 60's.
- Named PGA Player of the Year for the fourth time to tie Ben Hogan.
- Registered his 15th and 16th "major championships" wins with a record fifth at Masters, and the PGA Championship for the fourth time. In other "major championships" events of the year, came to within one stroke of first place in British Open and two in the United States Open.